Exploring Academic English:
A workbook for student essay writing

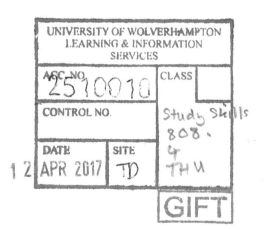
Jennifer Thurstun and Christopher N Candlin

National Centre for English Language Teaching and Research

MACQUARIE
UNIVERSITY~SYDNEY

© Macquarie University

Published and distributed by
National Centre for English Language Teaching and Research
Macquarie University
Sydney NSW 2109

Reprinted 1998, 2002

Thurstun, Jennifer
    Exploring Academic English: A workbook for student essay writing.

    Bibliography.
    ISBN 1 86408 374 3.

    1. Academic writing – Handbooks, manuals, etc. 2. English language – Grammar – Handbooks, manuals, etc. 3. English language – Rhetoric – Handbooks, manuals, etc. I. Candlin, Christopher N. II. National Centre for English Language Teaching and Research (Australia). III. Title.

    808.4

The National Centre for English Language Teaching and Research (NCELTR) is a Commonwealth Government-funded Key Centre for Teaching and Research established at Macquarie University in 1988. The National Centre forms part of the Linguistics Discipline within the School of English, Linguistics and Media at Macquarie University. In 1989, the National Curriculum Resource Centre (NCRC) from Adelaide was incorporated in NCELTR.

Sponsorship for the National Centre comes from the Department of Immigration and Ethnic Affairs (DIEA), the Department of Employment, Education and Training (DEET) and the Adult Migrant English Program (AMEP) at national and state levels, as well as from private clients and sponsors.

The publishers wish to thank Oxford University Press for permission to use concordances from the Microconcord of Academic Texts (Corpus B), 1993. All texts from which concordances in this book have been drawn are listed at the back of the book. The concordancing software used is Microconcord also published by Oxford University Press, 1993.

Acknowledgments

The research underpinning these materials was supported by the Macquarie University Teaching Grants held by the authors.

We would like to thank Tim Johns (University of Birmingham) whose work on the practical application of language corpora to teaching and whose generous advice during his visit to Macquarie University have been of great value in the development of this publication.

Diana Simmons assisted in the preparatory stages of the project and Siri Barrett-Lennard (Macquarie University) and Sally Burgess (La Universidad de La Laguna, Spain) and their students helped to pilot the materials. Robyn Woodward-Kron (University of Wollongong) and Carolyn Webb (University of Western Sydney) provided valuable comments.

The cooperation of all those involved has been greatly appreciated.

Jennifer Thurstun and Christopher N Candlin

NCELTR
Department of Linguistics
Macquarie University
Sydney
1997

Table of contents

Introduction for students

This book has been written to help you with your reading and writing at university. Whether English is your native language or your second language, you will find that there are differences between the kind of English you use in everyday situations, read in newspapers and listen to on the radio or television; and the kind of English you are required to read, listen to and write at university.

Most students find that through constantly listening to lectures, reading recommended texts and writing essays, by the time they have completed three years of undergraduate study they have finally learnt this academic language and can use it confidently. The units in this book will provide you with intensive exposure to some of the most important words used in academic English. So by working through these units you will gain the same exposure to these words that might otherwise take several years.

In these units, you will be looking at a small number of words in great detail. They are presented in authentic contexts which provide a rich experience of academic language, its grammar and vocabulary. The words have been very carefully chosen to make sure that you can practise and gain confidence with frequently used words to allow you to fulfil the various requirements of academic writing.

For example, you will be looking at how to use the words **evidence**, **research** and **source** in order to refer to the body of knowledge that already exists in a particular field. Then, when learning how to discuss the processes you have gone through in your own research, you will see how the words **identification, analysis** and **criteria** can be used. The words you study in this book should provide you with confidence in the basic vocabulary required for writing an acceptable academic essay. You will then, of course, be able to extend this basic list of useful vocabulary items yourself.

This method of learning and teaching has been made possible by computers and concordancing programs. A concordancing program can search through millions of words of text to find every example of a particular word (the key word), which it shows in its context. Key words can appear on the screen in one-line concordances, cut off at mid-sentence at each end of the line, or can be seen within a much larger context.

Reading a concordance

Before you start using these materials it is important to understand how to read a concordance. The computer, of course, is not concerned with meaning and simply cuts off the text where it has been instructed to do so. This results in cut-off sentences which may, at first, look confusing. However, once you learn to read a concordance, you will see that this is a very valuable method of discovering the meaning and use of a word.

In order to read a concordance effectively, you need to look at the words to the left and right of the key word. You will notice (in fact, it is useful to mark or highlight) the central group of words surrounding the key word which forms a phrase or can stand alone.

Look at the following concordance, where this central group of stand-alone words has been highlighted.

By underlining or highlighting the important, central group of words and noticing the words surrounding the key word, you are able to familiarise yourself with the way this word is used, its meaning and grammar. You would normally have to read a great deal in order to come across a word like **identify** eight times. With concordancing, the examples have been found for you and you can learn and discover in a natural way that is very focused and intensive. (The sign <p> indicates the commencement of a new paragraph).

```
ey do not rejoin. If we knew enough and could identify all the individual animals alive, say, one hu
st, policies must be changed. <p> We can only identify the proper criteria correctly if we accept th
 the therapist's role is to help the partners identify the problems that they face as a couple and t
ood is out of bounds in politics. It tries to identify the reasons which lead people to embrace this
hough less widely researched. Here, I want to identify one feature of that relationship which seems
r separate effects. Research was essential to identify the ill-effects attributable to each substanc
tion relative to that tradition. They hope to identify a coherent body of ideas which places them so
ndon School of Hygiene, where he continued to identify the chemical constituents of fungi and discov
```

Each unit will take you through a number of steps. Each of these presents a particular task. First, there is an explanation of the particular function of academic writing the unit deals with, indicating which three or four words you will be studying. Then, you will see some sample texts – full paragraphs taken from authentic academic writing – which use these words. You will then LOOK at a page of one-line concordance examples which use this word and FAMILIARISE yourself with its use by studying the concordance lines and doing your own guided research on the use of the word. This is followed by PRACTICE exercises to help you use the word correctly, and finally you will CREATE your own piece of writing, using the words you are studying.

Instructions for using this material

This material can be used for independent study, but since this approach to learning may be new to you, a few words of advice are important.

All the examples used in this material are taken from authentic academic texts from a wide range of disciplines that you may not always be familiar with. You will therefore find a lot of words and ideas that you may not understand, and it is important that you realise that you need not understand them all. Our concern is simply that you become very familiar with the use and meaning of the key words, with the patterns of language in which they are used and the kinds of words that are frequently found before and after these key words.

So don't worry if you find a lot of unfamiliar words here – just concentrate on the key word, its meaning, how it is used and the words often surrounding it.

The pathway for learning is as follows:

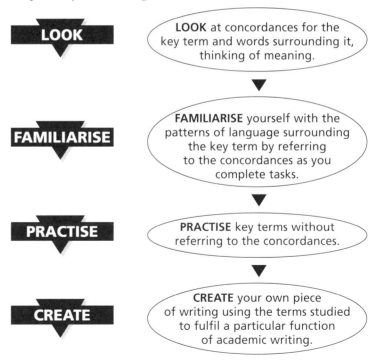

LOOK — LOOK at concordances for the key term and words surrounding it, thinking of meaning.

FAMILIARISE — FAMILIARISE yourself with the patterns of language surrounding the key term by referring to the concordances as you complete tasks.

PRACTISE — PRACTISE key terms without referring to the concordances.

CREATE — CREATE your own piece of writing using the terms studied to fulfil a particular function of academic writing.

Introduction for teachers

This project is designed to introduce students (of both English and non-English speaking background) who are new to the language used in universities to some of the most important items of vocabulary of academic English. Ability to use this vocabulary confidently is often considered crucial for academic achievement. A recent study (Bush, Cadman, de Lacy, Simmons and Thurstun 1996) shows that academics at Australian universities consider appropriate and accurate use of vocabulary to be extremely important, the basic concern being for clear communication rather than for the use of jargon and specialised vocabulary. Here we deal with frequently used words which are common to all fields of academic learning, leaving aside specialised vocabulary items associated with specific disciplines. The materials are designed both for independent learning and for use in the classroom.

The project uses an exciting innovation in the teaching of language, made possible by computers and concordancing programs. These programs permit the user to search millions of words of authentic language (in this case academic texts) for an indication of the frequency of use of particular words and word groups, and the possibility of viewing them in the context in which they occur. Concordancing has enabled us to present students with multiple examples of the vocabulary items in context, intensifying and compressing the exposure to these items which normally occurs over several years of undergraduate study. Students can examine these concordances to discover how they are used and to answer questions on their use. The presentation of concordances is followed by guided research and exercises enabling students to ensure that they are using the item correctly. (Answer suggestions are provided at the back of the book.)

The writing required of university students is particularly concerned with performing a number of different functions, such as stating the topic, reporting research, expressing opinions and drawing conclusions. Tim Johns from the University of Birmingham has made the point that students do not need to master a wide range of academic terms in order to write acceptable academic essays, but that they need to be competent users of a restricted set of vocabulary items and combinations for each function required in academic writing. This is a reflection of Michael McCarthy's advice to learners of vocabulary in general:

> There are many words you don't need at all and there are other words that you simply need to understand when you read or hear them. Finally, there are words which you need to be able to use yourself. Clearly, you need to spend most time learning this last group (McCarthy and O'Dell 1994:2).

With this in mind, we have chosen to concentrate on a restricted set of frequently used items of vocabulary for each of the following different rhetorical functions of academic writing: Stating the topic of your writing; referring to the literature; reporting research; discussing processes undertaken in a study; expressing opinions tentatively and drawing conclusions.

These materials have used the following concordancing program and corpus:

Microconcord. 1993. Scott M and T Johns. Oxford. Oxford University Press.
Microconcord Corpus of Academic Texts. 1993. Oxford. Oxford University Press.

Stating the topic

Issue, factor, concept

In the introduction to a piece of academic writing, and usually at a number of stages during the writing, it is necessary to make a clear statement of the topic of your writing or of a particular section.

Some words that you may find useful here are **issue, factor** and **concept**.

The sample texts on this page show you how professional writers use these terms. (Don't worry if there are words and ideas here that you don't understand – just concentrate on the use and meaning of the key words.)

When you have looked through the sample texts, work through the exercises to consolidate your understanding of how to use these terms.

Encouraging the family to discuss a particular current **issue** that it is facing is often the best way of assessing the **factors** noted above (Hawton and Catalan 1990).

The purpose of this paper is to examine a similar **issue**, the nature of sex determination, and the implications which attend a rethinking of the old certainties (Kennedy 1988).

Ultraviolet light has long been accepted as a provocative **factor** for herpes of the face and lips and many people find that their annual attack coincides with their visit to Majorca or trip to the ski slopes (Barlow 1979).

Three theses were presented as part of an explanation of the **concept** of authority. They are supposed to advance our understanding of the **concept** by showing how authoritative action plays a special role in people's practical reasoning (Raz 1986).

The **issue** for consideration is the selective treatment of disabled new-born babies (Kennedy 1988).

Part 1: Issue

Study this concordance, underlining or highlighting the central group of words that stand alone, as has been done in the first example. Then answer the questions which follow. You may like to look at question 1 before you start. (Don't worry that these are cut-off sentences – just familiarise yourself with the key words.)

```
itment was a major one. Social and economic issues and the representation of the users' point of vie
 of clerics and politicians on public moral issues and the subsequent failure to develop an ethos of
the developing countries that environmental issues are not conflicting but compatible with their com
nalty is relevant but not critical. The key issues are, on the one hand, the proper legal classifica
ethics, which concentrates on certain moral issues because of their political implications. A wo
 would not understand the complexity of the issues because of their poor understanding of Christian
If it is conceded that the really explosive issue concerns the homosexual, and that the situation of
that their sons are being conscripted. This issue evokes a blind anger against the English. The stre
uld not only affirm the fact that these are issues for all of us, but would also educate people as t
interventions focused on the most important issues for each patient. Therapists should also be flexi
nd respect for life. This is the particular issue for debate at this meeting, and I do not presume h
   a question of justice or fairness. The issue for consideration is the selective treatment of di
ion was discussed in Chapter 6.5 above. The issue here is whether provocation should remain a qualif
Control of protein synthesis is the central issue in cell differentiation and development. More accu
le. I also want to address two more complex issues in textual and sexual theory: firstly, the politi
ld War, when conscription was a contentious issue in Canada, it shows the orator as 'a country uncle
nd Britain, civil aviation remained a minor issue in the early years of the war. Nevertheless, the B
challenge for the 1990s. There is no single issue in contemporary human affairs that is of greater i
 It will therefore be seen that many of the issues involved here are similar to those raised by the
hreats against a person's property. Another issue is whether a refurbished general code of offences
ems natural to do the same for animals. The issue is philosophical, but it is so central to the anal
y'. There had been no agreement on the main issues of contention, but (aside from Canada) the Empire
tionalists should it have proven necessary. Issues of class conflict within the group were to remain
e, dominated by the great foreign political issues of the year, but there can be no doubt that Hitle
adopt appropriate measures to deal with the issue of climate change. This new interest is reflected
e morality of the many, particularly on the issue of the freedom of the individual versus the interv
o do – regard urban life as marginal to the issue of economic progress. On the contrary, they place
of 'positive contribution' raises again the issue of the social worth of sport, recreation and dange
 take more positive action to deal with the issues raised by the 1985 riots, but their experience ha
t; or what appear to them to be key ethical issues such as drink, tobacco, and money; or they may si
 the family to discuss a particular current issue that it is facing is often the best way of assessi
 in 1980–1, but in 1985 debate about racial issues was taken a step further. Peregrine Worsthorne, f
e of eventual self-government for India, an issue which threatened to be an explosive one for the Co
```

1 Which of the following statements do you think are correct? Tick your answer in the box.

An **issue** is a point about which there is some question, controversy, debate or doubt   correct ☐   incorrect ☐

An **issue** is a matter requiring thought or decision   correct ☐   incorrect ☐

The word **issue** is used when a matter has been shown to be true   correct ☐   incorrect ☐

2 Which *adjectives* are often used before **issue**? Group them according to whether they describe subject area, type/importance or quantity. The first has been done for you.

Group 1 (subject area)	Group 2 (type/importance)	Group 3 (quantity)
economic issues	_key_ issues	_single_ issue
_____ issues	_____ issues	_____ issue
_____ issues	_____ issue	
_____ issue	_____ issue	
_____ issues	_____ issue	
_____ issues	_____ issues	
	_____ issue	
	_____ issue	
	_____ issues	
	_____ issue	

3 Which *prepositions* commonly follow **issue**?

issue _for_ _____   issue _____   issue _____

4 Now list some of the words and phrases which can come after these prepositions.

the issue for _all of us_

the issue for _____

the issue for _____

the issue for _____

the issue in _cell differentiation_

the issue in _____

the issue in _____

the issue in _____

the issue of _contention_

the issue of _____

the issue of _____

the issue of _____

the issue of _____

the issue of _____

the issue of _____

5 (Note: To answer this question, look at your answers to question 4.)

Which of these prepositions is often followed by:

- people affected by the issue

- specific topics

- topics within which a number of issues are found

- time or place

- thinking and speaking processes

The issue _____ (people affected)

The issue _____ (specific topics)

The issue _____ (a topic containing more than one issue)

The issue _____ (time/place)

The issue _____ (thought/speech)

PRACTISE

6 In the following examples, fill the blank with the appropriate word. (Note: This is an extension exercise, not necessarily related to the concordance.) Choose from the following lists:

adjectives	verbs	prepositions
central	raises	for
religious	involved	of
particular	to resolve	

a Indeed, until the ecumenical era of the 1960s, few Catholics in Ireland were prepared to put before themselves some of the political and _____ **issues** which would have to be resolved if a united Ireland or accommodation to a separate political entity in Ulster were to become a possibility.

b The question of 'positive contribution' _____ again the **issue** _____ the social worth of sport, recreation and dangerous exhibitions.

c It will be clear from this that a proper approach will locate not only the appropriate level at which _____ issues, but also the appropriate problem-solver. This must be the person, body, or institution most qualified to deal with the _____ **issue**.

d This raises not only the **issue** _____ fairness or justice, but also that of selective treatment and respect for life. This is the particular **issue** _____ debate at this meeting, and I do not presume here either to pre-empt discussion or anticipate what I will say later when I consider it in greater detail.

e Control of protein synthesis is the _____ **issue** in cell differentiation and development.

f His speeches were, of course, dominated by the great foreign political issues _____ the year, but there can be no doubt that Hitler was deliberately steering clear of the 'Jewish Question'.

g This mediation of ethics makes indirect one's access to the problem of the relationship between the religious faith of some and the morality of the many, particularly on the **issue** _____ the freedom of the individual versus the intervention of the state.

CREATE

7 Now you can write a sentence or short paragraph in which you use **issue**. Imagine that you are writing the introduction to a section of your essay which deals with one of these topics:

- Whether marijuana should be legalised.
- Whether doctors should be obliged to prolong the life of a patient who has no hope of quality of life and who asks to be helped to die.
- Whether forests should be exploited.

Part 2: Factor

Study this concordance, underlining or highlighting the central group of words that stand alone, as has been done in the first example. Then answer the questions which follow. You may like to look at question 1 before you start. (Remember – just familiarise yourself with the key words.)

```
 health is the product of a combination of factors, among which medical care plays a relatively min
t show a rhythm that is dominated by social factors and the structure of our day. For example, coffe
 esteem, attitudes, leadership, and similar factors are of vital importance in any study of humanity
ot be regarded as a significant aggravating factor, but nor should the non-causing of death or injur
le down and problems occupy our minds. Many factors can cause this but one of them would be a body t
uses of deforestation. But these additional factors could eventually prove to be some of the most ha
 tasks are performed is affected by another factor -'fatigue'. This is a mixture of tiredness and a
e. Group formation may arise as a result of factors favouring defence or resource acquisition and th
r square metre of paddy surface. Additional factors found to affect the rate of methane emissions fr
ner's (1976) theory, the role of contextual factors had received little attention (but see Anderson,
  t of being a Jewish poet. Yet all these factors have influenced my work, usually without any eff
 origin is concerned, we shall take it as a factor in organic evolution, and shall content ourselves
relative importance of habit and biological factors in such circumstances is hard to decide. M
very rare event and certainly not a common factor in the evolution of animal traits. Characteristic
th your environment; by working on external factors in this way you will be able to work out practic
sychologists would rate as a very important factor in sex determination the role a person plays and
r bodies that are produced by some internal factor in addition to those produced by our environment
n the Christian tradition were not the only factors in precipitating the formation of the canon. The
me, the consequence is that the predominant factor in tropical deforestation continues to increase i
 the way policing is carried out is a vital factor in the context of urban unrest. An inquiry into t
ected by bombing more than any other single factor; nine in ten of those interviewed mentioned bombi
n that contextually mediated retrieval is a factor of general importance in associative learning and
me consciousness of the significance of the factor of time, was made by a late Zoroastrian priest re
k) than those determined mainly by external factors. Some of these points are illustrated in Table 3
dicts based on discriminatory or irrelevant factors, such as distaste for the defendant's background
 itself was explained by a variety of other factors, such as climate and population density. Montesq
dual. But the tests are susceptible to many factors that can distort the results. Each session norma
 role for generalisation decrement or other factors that might act by influencing the way in which t
ects. GOODE. I felt that there were several factors that caused him to want to continue living, and
 them in their susceptibility to contextual factors. The suggestion put forward by Kraemer and Rober
or management was an important contributory factor to New York's problems', and sought to apply the
d on only after careful screening. If these factors were absent, the question would be more difficul
t of complex political, social and economic factors which together create a predisposition towards v
bly longer in the female. There are several factors which help to prolong this period to perhaps thr
```

1 Which of the following meanings and uses of **factor** are correct or incorrect?

A **factor** is one of a number of elements which combine to produce a result   correct ☐   incorrect ☐

A **factor** is something which has been shown to be true and factual   correct ☐   incorrect ☐

A **factor** acts alone to cause something   correct ☐   incorrect ☐

2 Which *adjectives* are often used before **factor**? Group them according to whether they describe the subject area, type, quality/importance or quantity. The first have been done for you.

Group 1 (subject area)

_____ *social* factors

_____ factors

_____ factors

Group 2 (type)

_____ *similar* factors

_____ factor

_____ factors

_____ factor

_____ factors

_____ factor

_____ factors

_____ factor

Group 3 (quality/importance)

_____ *important* factor

_____ factor

_____ factor

_____ factors

Group 4 (quantity)

_____ *many* factors

_____ factors

_____ factor

_____ factors

_____ factor

_____ factors

3 Which *preposition* is most commonly found after **factor/s**?

factor/s _____

4 Write down the *verbs* which appear after **factor/s that** and **factors which**.

factors that *can distort the results*_____   factors which _____

factors that _____   factors which _____

factors that _____

5 Decide whether **factor/s** or **issue/s** should be used in the following sentences. (Note: This is an extension exercise, not necessarily related to the concordance.)

a The influences upon humans of the planets, moon, and _____ such as magnetic fields, atmospheric pressure, and cosmic rays have been imagined by some, including lovers, astrologers and those who, in the past, have diagnosed types of 'lunacy'.

b It will be clear from this that a proper approach will locate not only the appropriate level at which to resolve _____ but also the appropriate problem-solver. This must be the person, body, or institution most qualified to deal with the particular _____ .

c The _____ here is whether provocation should remain a qualified defence to murder, and, if so, how far it should extend.

d Even though biological _____ such as the state of hydration of the body will indicate that some food or fluid intake is required, the size and type of meal are likely to be determined also by habit and life-style.

e But the disorders cannot be fully understood unless they are seen in the context of complex political, social and economic _____ which together create a predisposition towards violent protest.

f His speeches were, of course, dominated by the great foreign political _____ of the year, but there can be no doubt that Hitler was deliberately steering clear of the 'Jewish Question'.

g Waking in the morning is again normally imposed upon us by social _____ – the need to get to work, to do shopping, to fulfil appointments, etc.

h This means that not only do we describe ourselves to ourselves and create identity constructs but we can also face the _____ of whether we want to alter those constructs and become another kind of person.

i Encouraging the family to discuss a particular current _____ that it is facing is often the best way of assessing the _____ noted above.

6 Now you can write a sentence or short paragraph in which you use **factor**. Here are some suggested topics, accompanied by vocabulary that may help you construct your paragraph.

- The causes of deforestation in tropical countries.
  - *logging*
  - *settlement*
  - *agriculture*

- Reasons for ill-health in remote communities.
  - *isolation*
  - *medical attention*
  - *information*
  - *physical conditions*

- Causes of poverty in developing countries.
  - *overpopulation*
  - *unemployment*
  - *education*

_____

_____

_____

_____

_____

_____

_____

_____

_____

_____

_____

_____

_____

_____

Part 3: Concept

Study this concordance, underlining or highlighting the central group of words that stand alone, as has been done in the first example. Then answer the questions which follow. You may like to look at question 1 before you start. (Remember – just familiarise yourself with the key words.)

ther primates. The capacity to form a **concept** of one's own identity and a process of comparison allo
e purpose of this book is to defend a **concept** of political freedom. It is only important to remember
can produce and reproduce. Ideas and **concepts** may thus be in fact misleading as to the real conditi
Faithfulness to the shape of common **concepts** is itself an act of normative significance. <p> Since
option by the Egyptians of a definite **concept** of time, although this may not have been consciously r
the Middle Ages developed no general **concept** of progress, many important innovations were made. Ind
he denial of the importance of ideas, **concepts**, and values for people, like the materialism of Feuer
ally, that it may be a flexible legal **concept**, it nonetheless is of a nature which does not extend t
ge as the one, already existing legal **concept** which has the obvious potential for expansion so as to
substantive existence but is a mental **concept** or means of measurement – a point of view that strikes
r were reacting against the mentalist **concept** that behaviour is caused by feelings, ideas, wishes, o
the Middle Ages. Moreover, our modern **concept** of history, however rationalised and secularised it ma
things out in their minds in terms of **concepts** and moral rules, and these concepts and rules were no
complexity explains why the system of **concepts** and of values has no direct relationship with the pro
d in part the historical formation of **concepts**, ideas, values, and institutions as a result of the l
m, but he also identifies three other **concepts** as essential to Conservative thought. The first is <i
have available to him Maynard Smith's **concept** of the evolutionarily stable strategy. If he had, my g
t how and why this atomistic temporal **concept**, which Buddhism used for its own purposes, was adapted
ronment. Piaget does not believe that **concepts** take their origin from linguistic structures. Rather
A voluminous literature on the **concept** of freedom has sprouted in the years since the publica
the Old carried implications for the **concept** of 'inspiration'. That the apostle Paul thought of his
of the Southern state along with the **concept** of the national entity, what that state goes on to do
obi session was with reference to the **concept** of core membership. In November 1988, thirty-two natio
s have changed, that's all. Where the **concepts** of God and Nature used to evoke a poetic response in
tical set of criteria adding up to the **concept** of adultery which allows hard problems to be solved wi
ce for any lengthy examination of the **concept** of justice. All I will say is that I reject as a model
sence of things is to be found in the **concept** of number, which was regarded as having spatial and al
ute Greek thinkers had found that the **concept** of time was difficult to reconcile with their idea of
o the burning debates surrounding the **concept** of natural selection. None the less, anthropology soon
plete agreement on all aspects of the **concept's** place and connections with other concepts. But there
egal rules failed to develop, but the **concepts** which provide the stuff of legal rules are equally il
s for divorce so as to reinforce this **concept** of marriage and, in the absence of birth control, to p
esources, the initial element in this **concept** of political economy, is in crisis. Every year an unsu
communities alone. The tree-planting **concept** has already been accepted in principle by the Intergov

Notice that the meaning of **concept** differs slightly from the meaning of **issue,** which in turn differs slightly from the meaning of **factor**.

1   When do you think you would use the word **concept**?

To refer to a mental picture or image   correct ☐   incorrect ☐

To refer to a thought or idea   correct ☐   incorrect ☐

To indicate that there is some controversy or argument
 regarding a matter   correct ☐   incorrect ☐

2   List some *verbs* that are often used before **concept**. The first has been done for you.

_____*to form*___ a concept   _____ three other concepts

_____ a concept   _____ concepts

_____ in the concept   _____ the concept

_____ the concept   _____ this concept

                                                         _____ no general concept

3   List some *adjectives* that are commonly used before **concept**. The first has been done for you.

_____*common*___ concepts   _____ concept

_____ concept   _____ concept

_____ concept   _____ concepts

_____ concept   _____ concept

_____ concept   _____ concept

4 Which word is most commonly used after **concept**?

concept _____

5 Write down examples of expressions that can follow **a concept of**.

a concept of _one's own identity_____

a concept of _____

a concept of _____

a concept of _____

a concept of _____

a concept of _____

a concept of _____

a concept of _____

a concept of _____

a concept of _____

a concept of _____

a concept of _____

a concept of _____

a concept of _____

a concept of _____

a concept of _____

a concept of _____

6 Decide which words to use in the blanks in the following examples. Choose from the words below. (Note: The following are extension exercises, not necessarily related to the concordance.)

adjectives   *verbs*
legal   to defend
mental   to form
modern
definite
new

a Our _____ **concept** of history, however rationalised and secularised it may be, still rests on the concept of historical time which was inaugurated by Christianity.

b The capacity _____ a **concept** of one's own identity and a process of comparison allowing an estimation of one's esteem among one's fellows that affects one's view of oneself are central features of humanity.

c According to this definition, time has no substantive existence but is a _____ **concept** or means of measurement – a point of view that strikes us today as being remarkably modern.

d One may even say that the whole purpose of this book is _____ a **concept** of political freedom.

e If this is the case, rather than attempt to invent a _____ conceptual framework, there is much to be said for turning to marriage as the one, already existing _____ **concept** which has the obvious potential for expansion so as to provide the institutional framework for such a union.

f As S.G.F. Brandon has pointed out, the great popularity of the cult of Osiris meant, in effect, the adoption by the Egyptians of a _____ **concept** of time, although this may not have been consciously recognised.

7 Draw a line matching each part of a sentence on the left hand side with its corresponding part on the right.

Piaget does not believe that concepts	factor governing the doctor-patient relationship.
The other single most important	of God and Nature used to evoke a poetic response in the nineteenth-century reader, the modern poets rely on sex and myth to produce the same effect.
The issue here is	whether provocation should remain a qualified defence to murder and, if so, how far it should extend.
Another unifying principle is said to be the concept of trust. This, it is said, is the key	take their origin from linguistic structures.
Where the concepts	issue in the early years of the war.
With the conduct of hostilities the paramount concern for both the USA and Britain, civil aviation remained a minor	factor responsible for raising the standard of care was the recognition of venereology as a clinical speciality in its own right.

CREATE

8 Now you can use the following information to create your own introductory paragraph to an essay entitled *Should developed countries subsidise developing countries in order to prevent further deforestation?*

Issues
- Rapid deforestation in tropical countries
- Global warming
- Death of birds, animals and insects dependent on forests
- Medicinal properties of plants found in forests

Factors contributing to deforestation in developing countries
- Overpopulation
- Poverty
- Foreign debt
- Need for agricultural expansion
- Demand for timber
- High price of timber

Concept
- Responsibility of developed countries to safeguard the world's environment

_____

_____

_____

_____

_____

_____

_____

_____

_____

_____

Referring to the literature

Evidence, research, source

When writing or speaking about the body of knowledge that exists in a certain area of learning, it is important that you refer to the published literature. In order to do this effectively, you will need terms to describe this body of knowledge.

In this unit you will look in detail at the use of three frequently used terms: **evidence**, **research** and **source**.

The sample texts on this page show you how professional writers use these terms. (Remember don't worry if there are words and ideas here that you don't understand – just concentrate on the use and meaning of the key words.) When you have looked at the sample texts, work through these exercises to consolidate your understanding of how to use these terms.

Axelrod draws a moving illustration of the importance of the shadow of the future from a remarkable phenomenon that grew up during the First World War, the so-called live-and-let-live system. His **source** is the **research** of the historian and sociologist Tony Ashworth. It is quite well known that at Christmas British and German troops briefly fraternised and drank together in no-man's-land. Less well known, but in my opinion more interesting, is the fact that unofficial and unspoken non-aggression pacts, a 'live-and-let-live' system, flourished all up and down the front lines for at least two years starting in 1914 (Dawkins 1985).

The idea of the *Umwelt* has re-emerged in ethology in Griffin's book. The *question of animal awareness* (1976), in which he argues that recent **research** in animal orientation, navigation, and social communication implies cognitive processes of a high order and even mental experiences of them. Griffin, whose own contribution to the experimental investigation of bird navigation and bat orientation is immense, argues that the objectifying abstractions of both behaviourist learning theory and much contemporary ethology simply ignore these issues (Crook 1985).

Engels does introduce into *The Origin* some types of **evidence** for early family forms other than terminology. For example, in the fourth edition of *The Origin* he introduced **evidence** of group marriages occurring among the Australian Aborigines. Unfortunately this type of **evidence** is also misleading, for two reasons. First, Engels believed that his **source**, the writers Fison and Howitt, provided independent **evidence** of group marriage, while in fact they too were enthusiastic supporters of Morgan's theories. Secondly, even though group weddings do occur, for example among people like the Samburu of East Africa, where traditionally all the young men of the same age group married on the same day a group of girls, this does not mean that the marriages are any less individual affairs for having been celebrated all at the same time (Bloch 1984).

Part 1: Evidence

Study this concordance, underlining or highlighting the central group of words that stand alone, as has been done in the first example. Then answer the questions which follow. You may like to look at question 1 before you start. (Don't worry that these are cut-off sentences – just familiarise yourself with the key word.)

may object that in the absence of conclusive **evidence** and analyses, one should stick with lower est
e have already seen, however, that on present **evidence**, and on the basis of extensive efforts at mod
t they contented themselves with the material **evidence** available in the form of bones and artefacts,
in science is open-ended and self-correcting. **Evidence** bearing upon it will be finely sifted. Some p
assed to both daughter cells. More conclusive **evidence** comes from experiments in which the nucleus i
ange, accounts of animal studies that provide **evidence** concerning the psychobiological 'platform' fr
> Weismann did offer some direct experimental **evidence** for the non-inheritance of acquired character
only retrospectively and such experience, as **evidence** for the existence of mind, can appear only as
es and substances are needed. But this is not **evidence** for an additional hereditary mechanism. Hered
ent, the conference focused on the scientific **evidence** for, the impacts of, and policy responses to
l artefacts of cultural success, and he gives **evidence** from several areas of mental health and educa
the causality of the correlations found. Some **evidence** may consist of tightly controlled laboratory
e incorporation of new material. Some of this **evidence** may be factual: the occurrence of certain fos
other apostles in comparison. Thomas demanded **evidence**. Nothing is more lethal for certain kinds of
) study of the lion pride. These animals show **evidence** of considerable kin selection in that the fem
personal adjustment of each individual gives **evidence** of this, both at the level of the unconscious
with no cortex is a vegetable. There is clear **evidence** of localisation of function in the cortex. In
of this book was published. Indeed the recent **evidence** on plasmids can be seen as beautiful supporti
on. It is therefore interesting that there is **evidence** that the brain is remarkably good at recognis
hough not exactly, uniform rate. However, the **evidence** that has finally convinced me that the neutra
only of parthenogenetic females. But there is **evidence** that species which wholly abandon sex are sho
spots scare off predators, and there is some **evidence** that this is so. But even if this adaptive ex
cs through many cell divisions. There is good **evidence** that the differences between them are not cau
ute with impunity unless there is categorical **evidence** that you are swelling hospital waiting lists.
is likely to be driven extinct. There is some **evidence** that wild populations of mice have, in the pa
We are not yet sure how far this is true. The **evidence** that has led people to think that it may be c
of a new rain forest.... Despite all the **evidence**, the World Bank has not yet accepted that the
ain kinds of meme than a tendency to look for **evidence**. The other apostles, whose faith was so stron
es) by refusing to speak, there is not enough **evidence** to convict either of them of the main crime,
dogma is of course a theory, but there is no **evidence** to suggest that it is wrong. The irreversible
best-judgment affair based on all available **evidence**, with varying degrees of demonstrable validit

1 Which of the following meanings of **evidence** do you think are correct? Tick your answer in the box.

Information indicating that something is or may be true	correct ☐	incorrect ☐
A single study that has been done	correct ☐	incorrect ☐
The origin of certain information	correct ☐	incorrect ☐
A judgment in a court of law	correct ☐	incorrect ☐

2 Are these statements correct? Tick your answer in the box.

Evidence is a collective (uncountable) noun	correct ☐	incorrect ☐
Evidence can be used in the plural form, *evidences*	correct ☐	incorrect ☐
Evidence can be used in the singular form, *an evidence*	correct ☐	incorrect ☐

3 Look at the concordance and list some *adjectives* that are commonly used before the word **evidence**.
Group them according to what they tell about the evidence. (The first in each group has been done for you.)

Group 1 (type/quality)	Group 2 (quantity)	Group 3 (time sequence)
conclusive evidence	enough evidence	present evidence
_____ evidence	_____ evidence	_____ evidence
_____ evidence	_____ evidence	
_____ evidence		
_____ evidence		
_____ evidence		
_____ evidence		
_____ evidence		

4 List some *verbs* that are commonly used <u>before</u> and directly <u>after</u> **evidence**. (Two examples have been done for you.)

provide evidence	evidence _bearing (upon)_	
_____ evidence	evidence _____	
_____ evidence	evidence _____	
_____ evidence	evidence _____	
_____ evidence	evidence _____	
_____ evidence	evidence _____	
_____ evidence	evidence _____	
_____ evidence		

5 List some *prepositions* that often come after the word **evidence**. (The first has been done for you.)

evidence _for_ _____   evidence _____

evidence _____   evidence _____

6 Look again at the concordance examples to decide which *preposition* (*for, from, of* or *on*) provides the following meanings?

meaning		*preposition*
evidence indicating	= evidence _____	
evidence to support	= evidence _____	
evidence relating to	= evidence _____	
evidence which has come from	= evidence _____	

7 In the following examples, fill the blank with an appropriate word. (Note: This is an extension exercise, not necessarily related to the concordance.) The first two examples have been done for you. Choose from the following lists:

verb	preposition	conjunction
provide	of	that
may consist	from	
may be		
to suggest		
comes		

a The central dogma is of course a theory, but there is no evidence ___*to suggest*___ that it is wrong.

b There are several lines ___*of*___ evidence. The simplest is that, if we look at cell division, we see that identical sets of chromosomes are being passed to both daughter cells. More conclusive evidence _____ from experiments in which the nucleus is removed from a fertilised egg.

c Arguments stand or fall by their plausibility according to the effective use _____ evidence; advance in theory is achieved primarily through the incorporation of new material. Some of this evidence _____ factual.

d It is therefore interesting that there is evidence _____ the brain is remarkably good at recognising patterns of similar marks.

e Some evidence _____ of tightly controlled laboratory experiments on motivational systems or genetics.

f There is good evidence _____ the differences between them are not caused by differences between the DNA sequence of their genes.

g There is some evidence _____ wild populations of mice have, in the past, gone extinct through epidemics of *t* genes.

h These animals show evidence _____ considerable kin selection.

i They include current selection theory describing the mechanisms of biological change, accounts of animal studies that _____ evidence concerning the psychobiological 'platform' from which human life ascended.

j We can suggest that the eye spots scare off predators, and there is some evidence _____ this is so.

CREATE

8 Now you can use **evidence** yourself. Read the following passages, then summarise them using the guides provided. (Although you are not expected to mention sources in this exercise, remember that correct referencing is essential when you summarise information for an essay.)

> The Greek community in Australia is often cited as a community that has had considerable success in maintaining its language. Tamis (1990), in a study on language maintenance in Australia, found that ethnicity and language were core values inextricably linked together for his subjects. The fact that the Greek language was maintained during 500 years of Turkish occupation says a lot for its quality as a core value throughout the history of the Greek people (Thurstun 1993).

Evidence from Australia _____

_____

> One further method of tension reduction which is of interest has been described by Graff and Mallin (1976). They found that in some patients, self-cutting could be prevented by the provision of physical contact by a therapist, such as in putting an arm round a patient (Hawton and Catalan 1990).

There is _____ that _____

_____

Part 2: Research

Study this concordance, underlining or highlighting the central group of words that can stand alone, as has been done in the first example. Then answer the questions. (Remember – just familiarise yourself with the key word, thinking about your answer to question 1.)

```
the idea that one could do genuine historical research about the Past. Nevertheless, by the latter p
uture must clearly be expanding international research and monitoring efforts. But this should not b
t was in fact academically isolated, and such research as might be undertaken had no facility for di
    t recent studies. Wrangham's (1975, 1977) research at the Gombe Stream reserve, a locality origi
of collaboration in mammals comes from recent research by Olwyn Rasa (1977) on the dwarf mongoose (
es under ecological constraint. A mountain of research has shown that the population of a species is
ditional funds will be required: to subsidise research in environmental problems for the developing
ting, the answer is also yes. However, recent research indicates that the slim person is not necessa
ons of emissions in this area, and additional research into non-intensive methods of agriculture sho
on of professional soldiers, he had created a research laboratory and clinic at St Mary's Hospital
ber of avenues which historical and aesthetic research might pursue, or at least it offers a way of
he more marked the effects of starvation. The research of the great ecologist David Lack (1954) show
d live-and-let-live system. His source is the research of the historian and sociologist Tony Ashwort
nly a few of these birds but Brosset's (1978) research on the Malimbus weavers of the Gabon
e problem at this point; far more comparative research on specific rice-growing and livestock-manage
  degree of inclusive fitness for all parties. Research on these animals is continuing. Among pri
ively little analytical work and virtually no research on building types or functions. We would make
antification, should be subject to scientific research during the 1990s, but essential first
it will be interesting to see whether further research shows an extension of the behaviour to incuba
intended for those who desire preparation for research, teaching or criticism in the field of archit
s that this is not the case, but only further research will tell. For the moment I cling to the idea
```

1 Which of the following meanings of **research** do you think are correct? Tick your answer in the box.

Investigation of a particular subject area   correct ☐   incorrect ☐

Proof that something is true   correct ☐   incorrect ☐

A single study that has been done   correct ☐   incorrect ☐

A careful attempt to discover information about a subject   correct ☐   incorrect ☐

2 Can you find an example of **research** used as an *adjective*? Write it down with its surrounding words.

_____

3 Look at the examples in which the research of a particular person is mentioned. Write down three phrases from the concordance which mentions the person who did the research.

_____

_____

_____

4 What do you think the date indicates?

_____

5 Are these statements correct? Tick your answer in the box.

Research is a collective (uncountable) noun   correct ☐   incorrect ☐

Research is not usually used in the plural form, *researches*   correct ☐   incorrect ☐

Research can be used in the singular form, *a research*   correct ☐   incorrect ☐

Research can be used as an adjective   correct ☐   incorrect ☐

6 List some *prepositions* that are commonly used after **research**, including the object which follows. (The first has been done for you.)

research **about** the past _____   research _____

research _____   research _____

research _____   research _____

research _____   research _____

research _____   research _____

research _____

7 Look again at the concordance lines in which *prepositions* (*about, in, into, on, by, of, at, during*) are used and decide what each preposition is usually followed by. Choose from:

> the broad subject area
> the topic
> the person
> the place
> the time

Research about is followed by _____

Research in is followed by _____

Research into is followed by _____

Research on is followed by _____

Research by is followed by _____

Research of is followed by _____

Research at is followed by _____

Research during is followed by _____

8 List some *adjectives* that can be used before **research**. Group them according to what they tell about the research. (Some examples have been done for you.)

Group 1 (type)	Group 2 (quantity)	Group 3 (time)
historical research	_additional_ research	_____ research
_____ research	_____ research	
_____ research	_____ research	
_____ research		
_____ research		
_____ research		

9 List some *verbs* that can be used after **research**.

research _might be undertaken_   research _____

research _____   research _____

research _____   research _____

research _____

PRACTISE

10 Decide whether **research** or **evidence** should be used in the following sentences. (Note: This is an extension exercise, not necessarily related to the concordances.)

a There is clear _____ of localisation of function in the cortex.

b He effectively discouraged the idea that one could do genuine historical _____ about the past.

c A priority for the future must clearly be expanding international _____ and monitoring efforts.

d We must admit verbal reports of inner experiences of human beings as valid _____ for studies of consciousness.

e The medical school of St Mary's Hospital, like the other London medical schools, was constitutionally part of the University of London, but was in fact academically isolated, and such _____ as might be undertaken had no facility for difficult chemical investigations.

f Wrangham's (1975, 1977) _____ at the Gombe Stream reserve, a locality originally made famous by the pioneering efforts of Jane Goodall on the chimpanzee, has clarified many mysteries.

g Weismann did offer some direct experimental _____ for the non-inheritance of acquired characters.

h One of the most remarkable accounts of collaboration in mammals comes from recent _____ by Olwyn Rasa (1977) on the dwarf mongoose, which lives in colonies in arid parts of Africa, often burrowing a refuge in the base of a termitarium.

11 Now you can use these words yourself. Read the following passages, then summarise them using the guides provided. (Although you are not expected to mention sources in this exercise, remember that correct referencing is essential when you summarise information for an essay.)

> There are several studies which indicate that a high appreciation of one's language and culture does not necessarily correlate with motivation to learn or maintain that language. In Ireland (Romaine 1989) low appreciation of the English culture and language has correlated with the continued learning and use of that language, and the practical dying out of the ethnic language. Trudgill (1983 in Edwards 1985), found that despite positive attitudes to their ethnic culture and language, speakers of an Albanian dialect, Arvanitika, in Greece did not pass it on to their children. Bentahila and Davies (1992) found that although Berber families in North Africa expressed affection for their language, its loss did not imply for them a loss or change of identity, and was hardly even regretted (a father was more upset about his daughter wearing European clothes than forgetting her Berber). In all these cases, the usefulness of shifting to another language (for economic reasons and for 'opening doors') appears basic to shifting from a language which is valued but maintained only as long as it is of use (Thurstun 1993).

In summary, there is _____ that _____

_____

This is supported by _____ carried out in Ireland, Greece and North Africa.

> In Sumatra, MacKinnon (1974) found that the orang-utangs of an area moved into the nearby hills when the largest calling male did so (Crook 1985).

MacKinnon's (1974) _____ produced _____ that _____

_____

Part 3: Source

Study these concordances, underlining or highlighting the central group of words that can stand alone, as in the first examples. Then answer the questions which follow. (Remember – just familiarise yourself with the key word, thinking of your answer to question 1.)

Group 1

```
om Marx. Marx uses Morgan principally as a source about exotic societies. He does note, in the let
his came entirely from his anthropological sources and really reflects an old-fashioned type of ar
 of the consular jurisdiction, for various sources attest that the two jurisdictions coexisted. Th
 pattern as sale. Since Ulpian is the only source for this, conclusions must be limited to late cl
 is by Hippolytus, the document is a major source for early liturgy and is the first text to witne
c writer of about 200 AD. These are a main source for our knowledge of the history of Greek scepti
he so-called live-and-let-live system. His source is the research of the historian and sociologist
```

Group 2

```
ement to the text, probably had its actual source in Bruant's song of social protest, 'Ctier', an
 the process are surprisingly similar. The source of energy is sunlight. The transformation is car
rting and the search for heroes could be a source of anxiety and even distress to the more reticen
hat this was the site that had served as a source of the infection, which had presumably originate
          There are still further possible sources of deforestation, these being atmospheric and c
context-specific. But this is not the sole source of the loss because other subjects that received
obscurity of parts of scripture was also a source of embarrassment if one took the books collectiv
   y through lack of moral fibre. Another source of doubt about the validity of the dependence th
us chapter were united in arguing that the source of this interference is to be found in a loss of
tiating proper control over the use of all sources of radiation. The interactions of X-rays wi
in's overseas government expenditure was a source of intense debate at the time, and has remained
st stimuli thus has its origin in a common source (the associative strength acquired by stimulus A
n a human being and therefore represents a source of danger. What these firearms offences appear t
```

Group 3

```
These are all cereal products. Other plant sources are nuts, seeds, and pulses (peas and beans). I
nutrients to the paddy, and provide a food source for the farmer. It would be useful to know what
 need, on any diet, to stop mixing protein sources in this way. It is a thoroughly good idea in or
large because of the yolk which acts as a source of nutrients for the growth of the developing em
 vegetables, as most people know, are good sources of this vitamin. Frozen vegetables (such as pea
n intake. Most people know the main animal sources of protein and can reel off a basic list: meat,
ion units, to produce methane as an energy source and the residue from that process as livestock f
stimulating emissions from natural methane sources such as northern peatbogs and offshore hydrate
y could, none the less, be considered as a source of information about European society several th
r and starvation. The clergy were the only source of education apart from the 'hedge school' teach
e that Renoir had been Lautrec's immediate source of inspiration: 'Renoir, who at that time had a
```

FAMILIARISE

1 Notice that the meaning of **source** in each of the three concordances differs slightly. Which meaning corresponds to the correct group? Tick your answer in the box.

	Group 1	Group 2	Group 3
Origin	☐	☐	☐
A writer, statement, book, person or document(s) supplying information	☐	☐	☐
A provider	☐	☐	☐

2 Look at the *prepositions* which follow **source** and decide whether the following statements are correct or incorrect. Tick your answer in the box.

Of is the most commonly used preposition following **source**   correct ☐   incorrect ☐

Of is not used when the meaning of **source** is 'supplier of information'   correct ☐   incorrect ☐

3 List some *adjectives* that can be used before **source(s)**, according to meaning groups.

Group 1 (supplier of information)	Group 2 (origin)	Group 3 (provider)
_____ sources	_____ source	_____ sources
_____ sources	_____ sources	_____ source
_____ source	_____ source	_____ sources
_____ source	_____ source	_____ sources
_____ source	_____ sources	_____ sources
	_____ source	_____ source
		_____ sources
		_____ source
		_____ source

Notice that most of the adjectives used in Group 3 specify the type of source, while most adjectives in Groups 1 and 2 indicate the number or importance of the sources.

4 In the following examples, fill the blank with an appropriate word. (Note: The following are extension exercises, not necessarily related to the concordances.) Choose from the following list:

another
animal
energy
principal
plant
only
possible

a Most people know the main _____ **sources** of protein and can reel off a basic list: meat, fish, eggs and dairy products such as milk, yogurt and cheese.

b Alternatively, using crop residues in bio-gasification units, to produce methane as an _____ **source** and the residue from that process as livestock feed or fertiliser, might be an efficient way to use them in many developing countries.

c The clergy were the _____ **source** of education apart from the 'hedge school' teachers (Dowling 1968).

d There are still further _____ **sources** of deforestation, these being atmospheric and climatic in nature.

e _____ **source** of irritation to my father – of which we three boys were all guilty – was our aversion to visiting the barber often enough to satisfy him.

f Examples of _____ **sources** of protein are bread, rice, spaghetti, and breakfast foods like porridge, Weetabix and Shredded Wheat. These are all cereal products. Other _____ **sources** are nuts, seeds and pulses (peas and beans). If you consume a mixture of _____ **sources** of protein (such as a cereal product with nuts, seeds or pulses) then you will have a good mix of the kinds of building bricks (amino acids) that the body requires.

g These translations, and the commentaries which they provoked, constituted the _____ **source** of informed Western knowledge of Islam until the sixteenth century.

5 In each concordance grouping below, one of the words you have studied in this unit is missing. Decide which word is needed for each group and write it on the line provided.

Group 1

```
        studies. Wrangham's (1975, 1977)          at the Gombe Stream reserve, a locality o
  of inclusive fitness for all parties.           on these animals is continuing. Among
  missions in this area, and additional           into non-intensive methods of agriculture
  w of these birds but Brosset's (1978)           on the Malimbus weavers of the G
   who, like myself had conducted field           in Africa, I undertook a survey of existi
```

Group 2

```
   dgment affair based on all available           with varying degrees of demonstrable vali
  of the lion pride. These animals show            of considerable kin selection in that the
        News reports a 'growing body of            that intentionally lit fires over the glo
  s of course a theory, but there is no             to suggest that it is wrong. The irrevers
  gh many cell divisions. There is good             that the differences between them are not
```

Group 3

```
  ents to the paddy, and provide a food            for the farmer. It would be useful to kn
  ciency in competition is thus a prime             of selection and occurs in many aspects o
  nits, to produce methane as an energy             and the residue from that process as live
  e Christian doctrine the flesh is the             of evil and the soul or mind is elevated
        eleases. The largest agricultural           of methane production is anaerobic bacter
```

6 Draw a line matching each part of a sentence on the left hand side with its corresponding part on the right.

Recent research	such a process of group selection seems unlikely to be important in evolution.
There are still further possible sources	needs to be done, enough is known to make preliminary suggestions.
We have already seen, however, that on present evidence,	indicates that the slim person is not necessarily eating in a way to promote maximum health.
These are a main	research of the historian Tony Ashworth.
His source is the	comes from experiments in which the nucleus is removed from a fertilised egg.
While much more research	source for our knowledge of the history of deforestation.
More conclusive evidence	of deforestation, these being atmospheric and climatic in nature.

7 Decide whether the missing word in these concordance lines is **research**, **evidence** or **source(s)**. The first is done for you.

unreasonably see in these actions the _evidence_ of communal meal-taking in man and its im

experiences of human beings as valid _____ for studies of consciousness. Contemporar

,who like myself had conducted field _____ in Africa, I undertook a survey of existi

st clearly be expanding international _____ and monitoring efforts. But this should n

helpful, however, in a search for the _____ and significance of our social organizati

boration in mammals comes from recent _____ by Olwyn Rasa (1977) on the dwarf mongoos

d countries unable to borrow from any _____ without the IMF 'seal of approval' must u

ere as N20 ,/i.) ,p. While much more _____ needs to be done to determine which ferti

on fossil fuels as a principal energy _____ in the future, along with continued defor

y relatively little has been spent on _____ and development on these technologies, co

marked the effects of starvation. The _____ of the great ecologist David Lack (1954)

strially developed world are the main _____ of greenhouse gases and therefore bear th

8 Now you can use these words yourself. Read the following passages, then summarise them, using the guides provided. (Although you are not expected to mention sources in this exercise, remember that correct referencing is essential when you summarise information for an essay.)

> Fox refers to an old Welsh poem, ascribed to a bard named Llarwarch Hen, which describes, in vivid language, the destruction of a city on the Welsh border and the slaughter of the chief to whom the city belonged. This mention of a poem may have given Owen the idea for a poem of his own (Stallworthy 1977).

The source of Owen's poem may have been _____

_____

> Now, there are problems with the simple postulation of a link between unemployment, crime and disorder, as Mrs. Thatcher is only too willing to point out. There is an enormous literature of research on the relationship, which the late Steven Box (1987) has usefully summarised and reviewed in his very important last book, *Recession, Crime and Punishment*. (MacGregor and Pimlott 1991).

Box (1987) has _____

_____

> Generally he (Marx) seems to have synthesized the Inca and oriental date, and he used information from Prescott to explain the working of the "Asiatic" mode of production (Bloch 1984).

Marx used Prescott as a _____

_____

> Hall and Honey (1987) report a study which indicates that appropriate contextual clues must be present for satisfactory retrieval of the effects of initial conditioning (Hall 1991).

There is some _____ to _____ that _____

_____

> The survey on which the original report, and hence this chapter, was based was perforce undertaken as a 'desk research' investigation. While it drew upon the author's twenty years of travel and work throughout the boime, it relied primarily on an extensive survey of the recent professional literature (Leggett 1990).

The main _____ of information for this chapter _____

_____

Reporting the research of others

According to, claim, suggest

When referring to previous work that has been done in a scholarly field, or when writing a literature review, it is important to use appropriate vocabulary. The terms **according to**, **claim** and **suggest** are extremely useful for reporting on the studies, experiments, reviews, ideas, articles and books of others.

The sample texts on this page show you how professional writers use these terms. (Don't worry if there are words and ideas here that you don't understand – just concentrate on the use and meaning of the key words.)

When you have looked through the sample texts, work through the exercises to consolidate your understanding of how to use these terms.

In pre-Christian antiquity two theories of inspiration were widely current. **According to** the first view, inspiration is an enhancement of natural, rational discernment, not a suspension or abolition. This view allowed room for disagreement between prophets and for the recognition of limitations in the human factor. **According to** the second view, inspiration was mantic possession: the divine afflatus took over the voice of prophet or prophetess, and employed the human agent as a musician plays a lyre which has no mind of its own (McManners, 1990).

Bacon was obviously an entertaining, civil, and witty personal companion, though he seems to have been somewhat cold-hearted and lacking in strong affection. He died, **according to** John Aubrey, the seventeenth-century biographer, as a martyr to the cause of scientific experiment (Woolhouse, 1988).

Although Barraclough's (1972) **suggestion** that as many as a fifth of the suicides in a series he studied might have been prevented by the wider use of lithium would be difficult to substantiate and is probably an overestimate, the fact that the lives of as many as 16 per cent of patients with manic-depressive illness may end in suicide (Pitts and Winokur 1964) **suggests** that lithium is likely to have an important role in the prevention of suicide in some patients (Hawton and Catalan, 1990).

Recent work **suggests** that there might be a daily rhythm in the composition of a mother's milk. Particularly in countries where the diet is poor it might be of very considerable significance if the mother can make better milk at some times of the day. There is still, however, disagreement between researchers as to when the mother produces the most nutritious milk. This might reflect cultural differences as well as effects due to the type and quantity of food consumed by the mother (Waterhouse, Minors and Waterhouse, 1990).

Though politicians often **claim** that the authority the law **claims** for itself is justified, there has hardly been any political theorist in recent times who has shared this view. It is, however, often **claimed** that there is a qualified obligation to obey the law, based on the authority of governments in just regimes, for so long as they remain just (Raz, 1986).

Part 1: According to

Study this concordance, underlining or highlighting the central group of words that stand alone, as has been done in the first example. Then answer the questions which follow. Notice that <p> indicates the beginning if a new paragraph. You may like to look at question 1 before you start. (Don't worry that these are cut-off sentences – just familiarise yourself with the key words.)

```
rely casual, but have historical substance. According to a basically Aristotelian view, science was
   significant feature was freedom from fear. According to a Sumerian poet: 'Once upon a time there wa
 f Germans (around a third of the population according to American surveys carried out in 1945) were
dequate because skies were so often cloudy. According to Asser's Life of King Alfred, that
ks by purely biochemical means. <p> Plants, according to Axelrod and Hamilton, may even take revenge
rsy instead of constructive argument. Thus, according to Bacon, that wisdom which we have derived pr
n opposition to Sceptics and Atheists'. <p> According to Berkeley, the usual combination of material
en of dawn, blue of night, and red of dusk. According to Bernard, van Gogh was enthusiastic about An
s a fitting symbol of his grand conception. According to classical myth, Hercules set the pillars up
the Winthrop laboratories three years earlier. According to Coatney, this discovery 'created havoc bord
am was carried by the first conquests. For, according to early medieval Jewish and Christian legend,
 of the presence of the pairing family, is, according to Engels, the beginning of history as underst
s formation to its destruction and rebirth. According to him the universe sprang from fire and will
 as a whole had never much appealed to him. According to his biographer Rawley, it was as early as h
till practised in his own day. <p> In time, according to Islamic tradition, mankind had strayed away
of an immaterial substance, a mind or soul. According to Locke, however, the question is 'what makes
   in this case, it is indirect. This stage, according to Morgan and Engels, is marked by the limitin
d escalating repression by the Nazi State – according to one calculation, roughly one in every 1200
eeks. And new hope – 'utopian expectations' according to one report – arose again following the anno
lacial periods over the past 160 000 years, according to recent polar ice-core studies. Total global
e categorical distinctions of our language. According to such a theory, if we, in English, call both
   produce generalisation decrement and thus, according to the account presented above, an overshadowi
            chapter. 8.1 Singularities. <p> According to the general theory of relativity, space-tim
ting Roman dates to those of the Olympiads. According to the historian Polybius, the founding of Rom
of the calendar in AD 1582 (see Ch. 8). <p> According to the Iranian scholar S.H. Taqizadah, a corr
= by virtue of geometry and demonstration'. According to the science of optics, light travelling fro
ry forest. This conclusion is questionable, according to the survey's findings. <p> For one thing, d
on earth, of the chosen people, Israel. <p> According to the theologian O. Cullmann in his book <i>
d interpretation of proactive interference. According to this alternative view, the target associati
   over 7200 kg of oil equivalent per year. According to World Bank figures, each inhabitant of the
```

1 Which of the following correctly explains the meaning of **according to**? Look at the concordance examples for help, then tick your answer in the box.

as a result of	correct	☐	incorrect	☐
as stated by	correct	☐	incorrect	☐
in a way that follows the rules of	correct	☐	incorrect	☐
in a way that is generally approved of	correct	☐	incorrect	☐
as reported by	correct	☐	incorrect	☐
as far as X is concerned	correct	☐	incorrect	☐
as proved by	correct	☐	incorrect	☐
in a way that agrees with	correct	☐	incorrect	☐

2 Look at the concordance examples. List the words that are commonly used after **according to**. Group them according to whether the writer is referring to a person, a theory/view or a document/report.

Notice that **according to** has three basic meanings:
1 as stated/believed by (a person)
2 as reported in (a document)
3 in a way that agrees with/follows the principles of (a theory, point of view)

Group 1 (person)	Group 2 (theory/view)	Group 3 (document/report)
according to _a Sumerian poet_	according to _a basically Aristotelian view_	according to _American surveys_
according to _____	according to _____	according to _____
according to _____	according to _____	according to _____
according to _____	according to _____	according to _____
according to _____	according to _____	according to _____
according to _____	according to _____	according to _____
according to _____	according to _____	according to _____
according to _____	according to _____	
according to _____		
according to _____		
according to _____		
according to _____		
according to _____		
according to _____		
according to _____		

3 Look at the lists you have just created. What does **according to** most often refer to?

_____

4 Which of the following statements are correct? Tick your answer in the box.

According to must be followed by a person	correct ☐	incorrect ☐
According to must begin a sentence	correct ☐	incorrect ☐
According to is usually preceded by a full stop or comma	correct ☐	incorrect ☐
According to must refer to a specific person, concept or object	correct ☐	incorrect ☐
According to (X) often begins a sentence	correct ☐	incorrect ☐
According to (X) can occur at the end of a sentence	correct ☐	incorrect ☐
According to never occurs within a sentence	correct ☐	incorrect ☐

5 Choose examples from the box of statements on the left and link each example with one of the authorities/documents/sayings/beliefs in the box on the right, using **according to**.

State them in two possible forms. The first has been done for you. (Note: These are extension exercises, not necessarily related to the concordances given.)

Statements	Authorities/Documents/Sayings/Beliefs
a mankind has strayed away from the religion of Abraham	recent polar ice-core studies
b Hercules set the pillars up at the Straits of Gibraltar	Islamic tradition
c methane's concentration in the atmosphere in 1990 was more than twice as high as occurred in previous interglacial periods	classical myth

Example

a According to Islamic tradition, mankind had strayed away from the religion of Abraham.

or

Mankind had strayed away from the religion of Abraham, according to Islamic tradition.

or

Mankind, according to the Islamic tradition, had strayed away from the religion of Abraham.

b _____

or

_____

c _____

or

_____

CREATE

6 Now you can use **according to** yourself. Consider the following statements by various authorities. Report each statement as you would when reviewing the evidence for an essay, using **according to**. Be sure to use your own words and refer correctly to your sources.

> Every year an unsustainable 50 billion tonnes of minerals are extracted from the earth's crust (Leggett, 1990).

_____

_____

> Thus, in summary, the first duty of a doctor is to listen to and respect the wishes of his patient (Kennedy, 1988).

_____

_____

Part 2: Claim

Study these concordances, underlining the central group of words that can stand alone, as has been done in the first example. (Note: You may need to end the grouping with THAT if the idea that follows is lengthy.) Then answer the questions which follow. Notice that <p> indicates the beginning of a new paragraph. You may like to look at question 1 before you start. (Remember – just familiarise yourself with the key words.)

Group 1

e world of baseball, although some authorities claim priority for an alternative connotation. The Am
tical freedom, is valuable at all. They do not claim that all those people who cherished liberty, th
udgment of the merits. <p> Nor does the thesis claim that authorities should always act in the inter
us with anything other than truth. <p> Locke's claim that prior to experience the mind is 'white pap
 criticism of him and the regime. The Fuhrer's claim that his work had been sabotaged for years, and
ena produced by the sun. <p> Gassendi does not claim, of course, that it is any more than a hypothes
ed during cleavage, thus supporting Weissman's claim. But his fellow countryman, Hans Driesch, was n

Group 2

nds of contemporaries. The Cordoban Paul Alvar claimed that the Muslims pretended to wage war 'as if
 are not striking. Sixteen years later, it was claimed that 'nobody in biomedical research wanted th
regate independently of one another, as Mendel claimed that they should. A number of rarer departure
stem, and bark together form one tree. Joachim claimed that there are, however, three distinct ages
eptible, whereas their Nyaya-Vaiseka opponents claimed that it is only an inferred concept because i
<p> Michael Heseltine (1987, p. 138) has since claimed that 'we set a new objective: to make the inn
onsider a paper of Stoyanov (1979) in which he claimed to have obtained a solution without singulari
 matter of indifference. Although the Gnostics claimed to offer a higher knowledge than the simple f
lf-organisation of a coordinate system was, he claimed, quite beyond conventional science, and requi

Group 3

        of justice. (pp. 327-8). Rawls, however, claims more than this argument establishes. He claims
e perceived by the senses'? <p> But Berkeley's claims that his Immaterialism avoided the scepticism
          the normal justification thesis. It claims that the normal way to establish that a pe
 'The truest Plagiarism is the truest Poetry', claims Thomas Chatterton, warming to Ackroyd's theme,
ples to those of capitalism, but which, Engels claims, actually represents a state of affairs which
ts beyond direct perception. But he is not, he claims, denying the world of common sense, not denyin
nd Titmuss, 1987, p. 9). <p> In spite of their claims ,'targeted' programs frequently miss some of
        ly considered. In fact, The Ecologist claims ,TFAP is not really concerned with forests at
nd this despite the fact that, as Ball rightly claims 'The radical restructuring of British politic

1 Which of the following statements do you think are correct? Tick your answer in the box.

To **claim** is to say something is true although you cannot prove it   correct ☐   incorrect ☐

To **claim** is to prove   correct ☐   incorrect ☐

To **claim** is to present evidence showing that something is true   correct ☐   incorrect ☐

A **claim** is a statement that something is a fact although others may not believe it   correct ☐   incorrect ☐

A **claim** is a true statement   correct ☐   incorrect ☐

2 Look at the concordance examples. Which word most frequently follows **claim**?

_____

3 Find examples where **claim** or **claims** are used as a *noun*. Write down the phrases in which they occur. The first has been done for you.

Locke's claim that   _____   _____

4 Which of the following statements do you think are correct? Tick your answer in the box.

Claim never occurs at the end of a sentence   correct ☐   incorrect ☐

When **claim** occurs at the end of a sentence, it is usually a noun   correct ☐   incorrect ☐

When **claim** occurs at the end of a sentence, it must be a verb   correct ☐   incorrect ☐

5 Draw a line matching each part of a sentence on the left hand side with its corresponding part on the right. (Note: These are extension exercises, not necessarily related to the concordances given.)

We may now consider a paper of Stoyanov (1979) in which	conventional science, and required a special biological force
He had an exalted idea of history that is well illustrated by	denying the world of common sense, not denying the reality of a world of directly perceived objects
Such self-organisation of a coordinate system was, he claimed, quite beyond	his claim that the historian's duty is 'to rejudge the conduct of men, that generous actions may be snatched from oblivion
The phrase seems to have originated in the world of baseball, although some authorities	claim priority for an alternative connotation.
Certainly, he is denying the world of the philosophers, a world of objects beyond direct perception. But he is not, he claims,	he claimed to have obtained a solution without singularities.

6 In the following examples, decide whether the missing expression is **according to, claimed to** or **claimed that.**

a _____ a Sumerian poet: 'Once upon a time there was no snake, there was no scorpion, / There was no hyena, there was no lion, / There was no wild dog, no wolf, / There was no fear, no terror.'

b Michael Heseltine (1987, p. 138) has since _____ 'we set a new objective: to make the inner cities places where people would want to live and work and where the private investor would be willing to put his money'.

c Plants, _____ Axelrod and Hamilton, may even take revenge, again obviously unconsciously.

d Joachim _____ there are, however, three distinct ages or states.

e We may now consider a paper of Stoyanov (1979) in which he _____ have obtained a solution without singularities.

f The overthrow of the gentile constitution, which occurred as a result of technological changes, and as a result of the presence of the pairing family, is, _____ Engels, the beginning of history as understood by Marx.

g The Cordoban Paul Alvar _____ the Muslims pretended to wage war 'as if by God's command'.

CREATE

7 Now you can use **claim** yourself. Consider the following statements by various authorities. Report each statement as you would when reviewing the evidence for an essay, using **claim**, **claims** or **claimed**. Be sure to use your own words.

> The style of the painting is difficult to analyse, because much of it was cut off by the framing of the photographs, and what remains is partly hidden by the objects in front of it (Murray, 1994).

Murray

_____

_____

> Even today, Canadians are not nearly as far away from the tradition of Victorian gentility as we imagine (Waddington, 1989).

Waddington

_____

_____

> It is possible to lose weight and not suffer a large drop in metabolic rate (Ashcroft and Ashcroft, 1989).

Ashcroft

_____

_____

8 Remember the first meaning of **according to** (as *stated/reported/believed* by) and think about its difference to **claim** (to *say something is true or is a fact, although you cannot prove it or other people might not believe* it).

What is the difference between:

According to the thesis, the government always acts in the interests of the people.

and

The thesis **claims that** the government always acts in the interests of the people.

_____

_____

9 Now write two paragraphs in which you refer to some authority **claiming** something that you wish to question or challenge.

a _____ claims that _____

however, _____

b _____ claims to _____

but, _____

10 Now write two paragraphs in which you include both **claim** and **according to**.

a According to _____ 's claim _____

but _____

b The claim that _____ is, according to _____

however _____

Part 3: Suggest

Study these concordances, underlining or highlighting the central group of words that can stand alone, as has been done in the first example. (Note: You may need to end the grouping with THAT if the idea that follows is lengthy.) Then answer the questions which follow. Notice that <p> indicates the beginning of a new paragraph. You may like to look at question 1 before you start. (Remember – just familiarise yourself with the key words.)

Group 1

```
h more than 3.5 h. Bond and Westbrook (1982) suggest that the source of the discrepancy can <pb n=8
        sian Sermons on Human Nature (1726), suggest that the structure of human nature is more com
pposite to those of capitalism. Marx seems to suggest that the gens can actually co-exist with <i> d
in human evolution. Trivers goes so far as to suggest that many of our psychological characteristics
ormance, and this prompted Robinson (1955) to suggest that pre-training might be ineffective when th
thropologists whom they read. Morgan seems to suggest, however tentatively, reasons why one stage sh
```

Group 2

```
n the learned safety hypothesis, Kalat (1977) suggested a revision which he referred to as 'learned
lly generally accepted was 753 BC, originally suggested by Varro (116-27 BC). According to tradition
nically decreasing for positive arguments. As suggested by Szekeres (1972), it is therefore possible
equate. <p> The pragmatic short-term remedies suggested by W.J. Wilson (1987) in his study of inner
mination. Some use has been made of a control suggested by Kurtz (1955), in which the subjects recei
cation, and it may be, as Gillian Skirrow has suggested for video games, that television can be more
ry admonitions of scientific management, Gray suggested improvements that would ease the housewife's
ided by the French philosopher Descartes, who suggested that there were mechanical forces which moul
med the core of the Maya almanac. It has been suggested that the reason for this choice may have bee
elease salicylic acid. <p> Bernheim's results suggested that he had found some substances which were
as been made by D.C. Heggie. It has even been suggested that many of the markings found on upper pal
instituted. In the United States reports have suggested that up to 50 per cent of cases of gonorrhoe
her possibility. Rosen and Thomas (1984) have suggested that repeatedly squeezing a small rubber bal
ast a third of hospital patients. It has been suggested that alienation from others (both staff and
ing in any of them. <p> The weaver bird study suggested that the motivational systems of individual
the pattern would occur spontaneously. Turing suggested that the concentration of the chemicals migh
uestion of youth unemployment. Hattersley had suggested that the riots were a 'direct product' of hi
```

Group 3

```
problem of bedwetting. <p> What all this work suggests is that the human's body clock and rhythms sh
with the potency of parody. <p> The biography suggests that Eliot was never to lose the divided sens
ugh the Commonwealth and Empire. This article suggests that the British hoped to create an internati
m Christ's Incarnation. Astronomical evidence suggests that this may have occurred in the first half
hargy and sluggish behaviour. <p> Recent work suggests that there might be a daily rhythm in the com
ially in southern Iran. In fact, the evidence suggests that at the time of the great debates over de
hrough the mass media. 'Realism', John Berger suggests, 'is a way of joining others' and 'a kind of
```

1 In everyday English, the verb **suggest** most often means: *to tell someone what you think they should do, where they should go* ... etc. In academic writing it does not have exactly that meaning. Which meaning(s) do you think it has? Tick those you find in the concordance examples.

To mention something for people to think about	correct ☐	incorrect ☐
To propose a new idea	correct ☐	incorrect ☐
To offer evidence for something	correct ☐	incorrect ☐
To hold a definite view	correct ☐	incorrect ☐
To propose something without giving proof or stating directly	correct ☐	incorrect ☐
To propose something as being possible but not definite	correct ☐	incorrect ☐
To offer information tentatively	correct ☐	incorrect ☐

2 Look at the concordance examples. What words typically follow the verb **suggest**?

_____   _____

3 Draw a line matching each part of a sentence on the left hand side with its corresponding part on the right. (Note: These are extension exercises, not necessarily related to the concordance given.)

Trivers goes so far as to suggest that many of our psychological

D.B. MacDonald has speculated on the difficult question of the origin of this view in Islam and

Alongside the standard sanitary admonitions of scientific management, Gray

What all this work

Bernheim's results suggested that he had found

In the United States reports have suggested that up to 50 per cent

It has been suggested that sleep is a time when brain activity changes from one of acquiring, interpreting, and acting upon information obtained from the environment

suggested improvements that would ease the housewife's workday and strain.

some substances which were good for tubercle bacilli

characteristics – envy, guilt, gratitude, sympathy etc – have been shaped by natural selection for improved ability to cheat

of cases of gonorrhoea in males may be symptomless.

to one of consolidating daytime memories

has suggested that it arose from a Muslim heresy

suggests is that the human's body clock and rhythms show several periods and that the combination of life-style and environment tends to accentuate one of these.

4 Decide which word or phrase should be used to fill the blank spaces in the sentences below. Choose from the following list:

according to
claim
suggested

a It has been _____ that alienation from others (both staff and patients) on the ward often precedes suicide (Morgan and Priest 1984).

b Locke's _____ that prior to experience the mind is 'white paper, void of all characters', and that all its ideas, the materials of knowledge, come from that source, had been made earlier by Gassendi.

c Rosen and Thomas (1984) have _____ that repeatedly squeezing a small rubber ball in the hand until this produces considerable discomfort in the wrist and forearm can also help.

d _____ Albert Speer, Goebbels referred around this time not just to a 'leadership crisis', but to a 'Leader crisis'.

e He had an exalted idea of history that is well illustrated by his _____ (*Annals*, iii. 65) that the historian's duty is 'to rejudge the conduct of men, that generous actions may be snatched from oblivion'.

f Only a minority of Germans (around a third of the population _____ American surveys carried out in 1945) were prepared to concede that the war was lost.

g The pragmatic short-term remedies _____ by W.J. Wilson (1987) in his study of inner cities and public policy in the United States could serve as one starting-point for discussion of policy in Britain.

h Acknowledging the problems inherent in the learned safety hypothesis, Kalat (1977) _____ a revision which he referred to as 'learned non-correlation'.

i This run of critical and box office hits prompted C.A. Lejeune, film critic of *The Observer*, to _____ : 'these Coward films are probably the nearest things we have to a valid modern school in British cinema'.

j _____ Berkeley, the usual combination of materialism and immaterialism leads to scepticism because of its 'supposing a difference between *things* and *ideas*'.

5 As we have seen in this unit, the three words/phrases **according to**, **claim** and **suggest** are all used to report previous research/writing or to associate ideas, findings, or results with other people, organisations, or events. Each of the words has its own particular grammar and each has a slightly different meaning.

We can summarise:

According to is the most neutral way to report.

Suggest personalises the report (that is, it expresses opinion) and can be tentative, but is still quite neutral.

Claim personalises the report more strongly. It indicates that the person making the claim wishes the reader/listener to accept the report as a true statement, but does not offer any proof.

Note: All three can be commented on favourably, with agreement, or unfavourably with disagreement or criticism.

Write a report of one paragraph for each of the above words and (a) disagree with what is being reported and (b) agree with the report. Choose any topic with which you are familiar.

a According to _____

but (disagree) _____

because _____

b According to _____

and (agree) _____

because _____

c _____ suggests that _____

but (disagree) _____

d _____ suggests that _____

and (agree) _____

e _____ claims that _____

but (disagree) _____

f _____'s claim that _____

is _____ and (agree) _____

6 Consider the following statements by various authorities. Report each statement as you would when reviewing the evidence for an essay, using **suggest, claim** or **according to**. Choose your terms according to the degree of neutrality, of personalising or tentativeness the statement seems to indicate.

> It may even be possible for background, contextual stimuli to interact with the pattern of nervous activity evoked by the target stimulus in the early stages of sensory or perceptual processing (Hall, 1991).

_____

_____

_____

_____

> Efficiency in competition is thus a prime source of selection and occurs in many aspects of social life (Crook, 1985).

_____

_____

_____

_____

In some cases bodies were covered with red ochre, which may have been intended to simulate blood, in the hope of averting physical extinction (Whitrow, 1990).

_____

_____

_____

_____

Encouraging the family to discuss a particular current issue that it is facing is often the best way of assessing the factors noted above (Hawton and Catalan 1990).

_____

_____

_____

_____

We can only identify the proper criteria correctly if we accept that medical treatment in general ought to be divided, for our purposes, into two classes (Kennedy 1988).

_____

_____

_____

_____

7 There are other ways of reporting previous research and writing. Look at the following examples. How could you rewrite the relevant section of these sentences, substituting the words in bold type for words you have studied in this unit? (You may need to make some minor grammatical changes.)

a The report **made it clear that** adequate safeguards and standards were necessary.

_____

_____

_____

b **His point is** that there are also molecular changes occuring which are not selected, because they have little or no effect or function. This view is still controversial, but I think it is winning.

_____

_____

_____

c The Greenpeace **conclusion is** that the goal must be elimination of fossil fuels from the energy inventory, and that that goal should be reflected in the target for the year 2000.

_____

_____

_____

d **My own view is** that these exceptions are so infrequent that they are not a reason for abandoning the neo-Darwinist mechanism as the one which underlies the vast majority of adaptive evolutionary changes.

_____

_____

_____

_____

Identification, analysis, criteria

At various stages of your writing, you are likely to wish to explain or discuss the different procedures that you have undertaken in your own research, or processes which have been undertaken by others in studies you wish to refer to.

It is helpful to be able to write confidently about **identification**, **analysis** and **criteria**.

The sample texts on this page show you how professional writers use these terms. (Don't worry if there are words and ideas here that you don't understand – just concentrate on the use and meaning of the key words.)

When you have looked through the sample texts, work through the exercises to consolidate your understanding of how to use these terms.

Another of the many **criteria** to be **identified** could be the subsequent or continuing costs, economic and social, of proceeding with a particular treatment (Kennedy 1988).

We can only **identify** the proper **criteria** correctly if we accept that medical treatment in general ought to be divided, for our purposes, into two classes (Kennedy 1988).

This fundamental difference with the position of earlier radicals required theoretical **analysis** in two areas. First of all 'society', as distinct from the State, had to be isolated and **analysed**, and secondly an attempt had to be made at understanding the evolution of society (Bloch 1984).

It has already been noted that obstructive attitudes can prevent progress in therapy, and that such attitudes can usually be **identified** by carefully **analysing** the patient's attempts to achieve goals and the reason for failure (Hawton and Catalan 1990).

Part 1: Identification

Study these concordances, underlining or highlighting the central group of words that stand alone, as has been done in the first example. Then answer the questions which follow. You may like to look at question 1 before you start. (Don't worry that these are cut-off sentences – just familiarise yourself with the key words.)

Group 1

e seen at puberty. The isolation and chemical **identification** of several sex hormones in the late 192
akhtin's method lies not simply in the formal **identification** of a genre or a subgenre or a chronotop
  established only after much controversy. Its **identification** was an early success of X-ray crystallo
o the production of muscle-specific proteins. **Identification** of the new muscle proteins was made pos
loration of their difficulties had led to the **identification** of two additional problems: <list> <ite

Group 2

ure of construction as a whole; the facts are **identified** by the principles that result. In
erapy, and that such attitudes can usually be **identified** by carefully analysing the patient's attemp
  occurrence of a linguistic form which can be **identified** as Arabic. Christianity had a similar cohes
existence. <p> Another of many criteria to be **identified** could be the subsequent or continuing costs
2 BC), who rejected the idea that time can be **identified** with any form of motion or change. For, he
1 Greek literature, can nevertheless still be **identified** as a distinctive and possibly definitive ge
operties. <p> Many more carcinogens have been **identified** since then. Some are mainly of laboratory i
runs of mutual recrimincation. <p> So, we have **identified** two characteristics of winning strategies:
ver the last three hundred years or so. It is **identified** by a series of political causes espoused by
orerunners of Islam. A later Muslim tradition **identified** the Rock as the point from which Muhammad a
ed by Levene's tetra-structure. The sugar was **identified** as either ribose or deoxyribose: for a time
random). Forty years later these factors were **identified** as bits of chromosome, and a century later
er supply 20 years or so before bacteria were **identified** as causing the disease. Lime juice was reco
 Up to five stages in the life cycle could be **identified,** each of which might respond to a different
r estimated eight hundred buildings have been **identified.** Her techniques and their results were by n

Group 3

ey do not rejoin. If we knew enough and could **identify** all the individual animals alive, say, one hu
st, policies must be changed. <p> We can only **identify** the proper criteria correctly if we accept th
 the therapist's role is to help the partners **identify** the problems that they face as a couple and t
ood is out of bounds in politics. It tries to **identify** the reasons which lead people to embrace this
hough less widely researched. Here, I want to **identify** one feature of that relationship which seems
r separate effects. Research was essential to **identify** the ill-effects attributable to each substanc
tion relative to that tradition. They hope to **identify** a coherent body of ideas which places them so
ndon School of Hygiene, where he continued to **identify** the chemical constituents of fungi and discov

1 Which of the following statements do you think are correct? Tick your answer in the box.

To **identify** involves naming   correct ☐   incorrect ☐

To **identify** involves describing   correct ☐   incorrect ☐

To **identify** involves deciding what something is   correct ☐   incorrect ☐

To **identify** involves recognising   correct ☐   incorrect ☐

To **identify** involves criticising   correct ☐   incorrect ☐

2 Which *preposition* most frequently follows **identification**?

identification _____

3 Look at the second concordance group with the key word **identified.** Notice that many examples of **identified** are preceded by part of the verb **to be** (*is, are, was, were, been, be*). Mark the things/objects identified in these concordance lines and write them down, deciding also whether the singular or plural form of **to be** should be used.

_____the facts_____(is/are) identified)   _____(is/are) identified)

_____(is/are) identified)   _____(is/are) identified)

_____(is/are) identified)   _____(is/are) identified)

_____(is/are) identified)   _____(is/are) identified)

_____(is/are) identified)   _____(is/are) identified)

_____(is/are) identified)   _____(is/are) identified)

_____(is/are) identified)

4 Now look at the concordance lines in Group 2 which do not use part of the auxiliary **to be**, and mark the objects identified. Who or what are the identifiers in these concordance lines? What are the objects they identify?

Identifier		Object
we	identified	*two characteristics*
	identified

5 Which of the following statements do you think are correct? Tick your answer in the box.

When part of the verb **to be** is used with **identified**, the person who does
the identifying is unknown   correct ☐   incorrect ☐

When part of the verb **to be** is used with **identified**, the object which is
identified precedes the verb   correct ☐   incorrect ☐

When the person who does the identifying is known, the auxiliary **to be** is not
used and the object which is identified follows the verb   correct ☐   incorrect ☐

6 In the following examples, fill the blank with the missing word. Choose from **identification, identify, identifying, identified, identifiable, identity.**

a The sugar was _____ as either ribose or deoxyribose: for a time it was believed that plant nucleic acids always contained ribose and animal nucleic acids deoxyribose.

b The importance of Bakhtin's method lies not simply in the formal _____ of a genre or a subgenre or a chronotope, but also in the connection which he establishes between internal generic form and external history.

c This, though it is everywhere as various and as changeable as the biographical time which Bakhtin finds in classical Greek literature, can nevertheless still be _____ as a distinctive and possibly definitive generic shift.

d If we knew enough and could _____ all the individual animals alive, say, 100 million years ago which were ancestral to existing mice, we would expect to find those animals all belonging to a single species.

e It may consist in a rejection of the notion that there are _____ stages, or that talking of stages is a useful way of visualising evolution.

f The isolation and chemical _____ of several sex hormones in the late 1920s and the 1930s had many practical consequences.

g Once it was recognised that any kind of cancer had an _____ cause, it was natural to try and determine the exact chemical _____ of the substances responsible (the 'carcinogens').

h Research was essential to _____ the ill-effects attributable to each substance and to devise means of protecting against them and of overcoming them.

i Once it was recognised that animals orient themselves in a variety of ways, the engineering approach was extremely successful in _____ the underlying mechanisms.

7 Now you can use these words yourself. Read the following passage. Then write a sentence referring to the passage and explaining in your own words what this writer identified in the chapter mentioned (Chapter X).

In this chapter I shall begin by briefly considering the (rather wide) range of interference theories that have been applied to latent inhibition. Having identified the most likely candidates I shall then consider the critical experimental evidence (which again derives from studies of the role of contextual factors). Finally, I shall attempt to devise a synthesis that can incorporate the successful features of several theoretical approaches (Hall 1991).

_____

_____

_____

Part 2: Analysis

Study these concordances, underlining or highlighting the central group of words that stand alone, as has been done in the first example. Then answer the questions which follow. You may like to look at question 1 before you start. (Remember – just familiarise yourself with the key words.)

Group 1

```
ndemnation but a fair amount of sociological analysis as well with the result that there is a lively
answer the second question first. If ethical analysis in this context does not help in the real worl
ion of earlier radicals required theoretical analysis in two areas. First of all 'society', as disti
erning the doctor-patient relationship. This analysis is equally flawed. First, to argue that each p
r word. Much that is presented as conceptual analysis is really much more and includes advocacy of p
indings. But rather than undertaking such an analysis it will be enough to demonstrate that this con
analysis may be pushed, and however much the analysis may be necessary to our understanding of the w
er location of power and responsibility. Any analysis must take account of this, by understanding an
clude in their political writings a thorough analysis of the evolution of society and of pre-capital
Garry Whannel traced four main themes in the analysis of football hooliganism in the popular press i
udy has meant that there has been hardly any analysis of the major constitutional questions which ar
sentations of sense-experience, and with the analysis of composite wholes into parts. Its interest i
son or ratiocination is, some explanation or analysis of it. According to this, ratiocination consis
 itself. <p> In this section I will offer an analysis of consent. I will then show, in the next sect
d ethnicity an aspect that is central to any analysis of the inner cities and of any ameliorative ap
uman ethology rooted firmly in the objective analysis of behaviour sequences and components. So, in
ows the study of animal behaviour through an analysis of the lawful relations between stimulus condi
gues. <p> In this chapter we will present an analysis of the colliding wave problem using a method t
istic theme in combination with a subjective analysis of its mood was a component of much of the lat
egories, and necessary tools in the critical analysis of television. It is the necessary end-point o
pportunity to develop an effective political analysis of a 'popular' film. But perhaps the critics h
imal. To this I would respond as follows. My analysis of the particular qualities of the institution
ich the patient's feelings develop. Detailed analysis of this kind should enable the most appropriat
bout nutrition is probably just a very basic analysis of an extremely complex process. However, here
 by reviewing this work before turning to an analysis of the relatively few further studies that hav
mptoms or signs of the disease, in the final analysis the diagnosis hangs on the identification of t
ploy well-established methods of comparative analysis, often based upon the principles of taxonomy <
ent as might be comforting to think. Careful analysis, the development of alternatives, the devising
urpose of the anthropological and historical analysis. Although the discussion of this process is be
rists with overwhelm any tendency to logical analysis. One might ask whether motorists are ever just
ts information on somewhere else for further analysis. <p> How far does what we know about neurones
```

Group 2

```
te until such time as more detailed data and analyses become available. The estimate is advanced her
mmunication). <p> One of the best-documented analyses of altruism and kin selection in group-dwellin
```

1 Which of the following statements do you think are correct? Tick your answer in the box.

Analysis means the separation and consideration of the
various components of a phenomenon   correct ☐   incorrect ☐

Analysis is only done by chemists   correct ☐   incorrect ☐

An **analysis** attempts to determine the essential features of a thing   correct ☐   incorrect ☐

The word **analysis** can be used for both the singular and plural   correct ☐   incorrect ☐

2 Look at the concordances and list some *adjectives* that are commonly used before **analysis/analyses**. Group them according to what they tell you about the analysis. (The first has been done for you).

Group 1 (subject area)	Group 2 (type/quality)	Group 3 (quantity)
sociological analysis	_____ analysis	_____ analysis
_____ analysis	_____ analysis	_____ analysis
_____ analysis	_____ analysis	
_____ analysis	_____ analysis	
	_____ analysis	
	_____ analysis	
	_____ analysis	
	_____ analysis	
	_____ analysis	
	_____ analysis	
	_____ analysis	
	_____ analysis	
	_____ analysis	

3 What is the *preposition* most frequently used after **analysis**?

analysis _____

4 What is the plural form of **analysis**?

_____

5 In the following examples, decide whether the missing word is **analysis**, **identification**, **analysed** or **identified**.

a Football hooliganism has been defined as a major social problem. It has attracted not only widespread condemnation but a fair amount of sociological _____ as well with the result that there is a lively debate taking place about its origins and nature.

b A later Muslim tradition _____ the Rock as the point from which Muhammad ascended into heaven, where he was guided by the prophets who preceded him, including Abraham, Moses, and Jesus.

c A close examination of these various experiments might reveal the reason for their discrepant findings. But rather than undertaking such an _____ it will be enough to demonstrate that this control procedure is in principle inadequate for our present needs.

d If this symptom is _____ closely, it will be found that it is 'external' in character.

e It has already been noted that obstructive attitudes can prevent progress in therapy, and that such attitudes can usually be _____ by carefully analysing the patient's attempts to achieve goals and the reason for failure.

f When the results were further _____, it was shown that this high incidence was largely due to the male homosexual population attending these clinics.

g _____ of the new muscle proteins was made possible by fusing human cells with mouse muscle cells; the human muscle proteins are similar but distinct from those made by mice.

h The first book where Marx and Engels include in their political writings a thorough _____ of the evolution of society and of pre-capitalist social formations is *The German Ideology*.

i Some people are more likely to develop these complications and can be _____ by demonstrating the presence of a particular tissue-type in their body make-up.

j The naturalistic theme in combination with a subjective _____ of its mood was a component of much of the later Naturalism of the 1880s, the decade that bridged the Realist and Symbolist movements.

k Forty years later these factors were _____ as bits of chromosome, and a century later as molecules of DNA.

CREATE

6 Now you can use these words yourself. Imagine that you have been asked to write a short essay in which you **analyse** the difficulties which many new students experience when commencing study in a university. Write your introductory paragraph, identifying the various difficulties that you intend to discuss.

_____

_____

_____

_____

_____

_____

_____

_____

Part 3: Criteria

Study these concordances, underlining or highlighting the central group of words that stand alone, as has been done in the first example. Then answer the questions which follow. You may like to look at question 1 before you start. (Remember – just familiarise yourself with the key words.)

Group 1

rply from the profane, they had no clear **criteria** to show where the line was to be drawn. What carri
own some, though not all, of the medical **criteria** for determining sex, and resolves that these crite
cular facts. Obviously, purely objective **criteria** such as the patient's age or the particular illnes
ave to do is to come up with some set of **criteria** which relate to the relative value we are prepared
ged. <p> We can only identify the proper **criteria** correctly if we accept that medical treatment in g
e the biological criteria. Psychological **criteria** are thus given no weight, despite the fact that th
g pus cells in the urethra, but the same **criteria** cannot be applied to the woman. One is left with e
        partners. <p> Darwin used several **criteria** for distinguishing sexual characteristics selected
ical issue, and decides that, of all the **criteria** involved, the crucial ones for determining how the
essentially heterosexual character', the **criteria** used to assess 'womanhood' must, Ormrod J. asserts
concern here, what are important are the **criteria** whereby resources are allocated. These have to be
ed above, 'I have not contended that the **criteria** of excellence lack a rational basis in everyday li
of religious knowledge and provided the **criteria** for distinguishing truth from heresy. Martin Luthe
countries would meet either of these two **criteria,** and that the total resources needed would be abou

Group 2

through some sign and whether we have a **criterion** by which we may recognise the sign and judge what
be evaluated. They do not have an agreed **criterion** of perfection that can be used as a principle for
mselves'; when they say that there is no **criterion** of truth, 'they are not speaking of what things a
many people, can in fact be taken as one **criterion** for human maturity. And such behaviour must of co
es, with few intermediates. The relevant **criterion** is whether two forms commonly interbreed in the w
used for the list of accepted books. The **criterion** for admission was not so much that traditions vin
role of sensory experience. For him the **criterion** of musical phenomena was not mathematics but the
n Chapter 1. Is there such a thing as a **'criterion'** of truth? Do we have any `instrument' or means o

1 Which of the following statements do you think are correct? Tick your answer in the box.

Criteria are standards by which something can be judged	correct ☐	incorrect ☐
Criteria are rules for testing something	correct ☐	incorrect ☐
A **criterion** is justified criticism	correct ☐	incorrect ☐
A **criterion** is a necessary feature qualifying something or someone for inclusion in a group	correct ☐	incorrect ☐
Criteria is the plural form of **criterion**	correct ☐	incorrect ☐

2 Look at the concordances and list some *adjectives* that are commonly used before **criteria/criterion**. Group them according to what they tell about the criteria. (The first in each group has been done for you.)

Group 1 (type/quality)	Group 2 (subject area)	Group 3 (quantity)
clear criteria	_medical_ criteria	_several_ criteria
_____ criteria	_____ criteria	_____ criteria
_____ criteria		_____ criteria
_____ criteria		_____ criterion
_____ criteria		_____ criterion

3 Which *prepositions* are most commonly used after **criteria/criterion**?

_____   _____

4 Write down the things being judged/evaluated/tested which come after the *prepositions* in the concordance examples.

criteria for *determining sex* _____   criteria of *excellence* _____

criteria for _____   criterion of _____

criteria for _____   criterion of _____

criterion for _____   criterion of _____

criterion for _____

5 Look at the lists you have created above and decide which preposition (*for* or *of*) is used when referring to:
mental activities
abstract things or ideas
acceptance into a group

criteria _____ mental activities

criteria _____ abstract things or ideas

criteria _____ acceptance into a group

6 Draw a line matching each part of a sentence on the left hand side with its corresponding part on the right.

They had no clear	of criteria which relate to the relative value we are prepared, if pressed, to attribute to a particular form of special treatment.
The relevant criterion	have any 'instrument' or means of getting at the truth?
What we have to do is to come up with some set	the patient's age or the particular illness cannot be justified or relied upon.
We can only identify the proper criteria correctly	is whether two forms commonly interbreed in the wild, and not whether they can be persuaded to do so in captivity.
This capacity for choice, implicit rather than active in so many people, can in fact be taken as one	criteria to show where the line was to be drawn.
Obviously, purely objective criteria such as	criterion for human maturity.
Is there such a thing as a 'criterion' of truth? Do we	if we accept that medical treatment in general ought to be divided, for our purposes, into two classes.

7 In each concordance group below, one of the words you have studied in this unit is missing. Decide which word is needed for each group.

the deathbed, so is it time for critical
t nutrition is probably just a very basic
alled it 'the most exciting and brilliant
the patient's feelings develop. Detailed
demonstrating its purity and getting an
s. <p> In this chapter we will present an
to a new environment. In fact, genetical
erative ability. The need for theoretical
m and dualist self-description) which, on

to pay attention to real people's lived
of an extremely complex process. However
of the ideological forces in conflict to
of this kind should enable the most appr
of the elements present. He named it 'nu
of the colliding wave problem using a me
of plant 'ecotypes' (i.e. populations ad
of many more cases such as the lion is c
simply appear as inherent properties of

one who by reference to purely biological
down some, though not all, of the medical
ng pus cells in the urethra, but the same
al evidence is that where the two sets of
that sensible qualities are not the sole
re the biological criteria. Psychological
the relative importance of solely medical
countries would meet either of these two
ent would be only one of several relevant

is undoubtedly of the male sex at birth
for determining sex, and resolves that t
cannot be applied to the woman. One is l
clash, the only effective treatment is t
of perceptibility and that time is perce
are thus given no weight, despite the fa
without giving any justification for his
and that the total resources needed woul
On this view, a doctor could avoid liabi

receptors for retinoic acid have now been
om). Forty years later these factors were
upply 20 years or so before bacteria were
y concerned with molecules which could be
otal number of attempted suicide patients
y, and that such attituded can usually be
d. In some of the cases new problems, not
ll vary according to the types of problem
oup at the Lederle laboratories which had

in the cells in the progress zone. All o
as bits of chromosome, and a century lat
as causing the disease. Lime juice was r
at the time, i.e. with molecular weights
on tha basis of general hsopital referra
by carefully analysing the patient's att
at the outset, emerged during the course
and the therapeutic approaches favoured
the structure of folic acid. The substan

8 Now you can use these words yourself. You have been asked to write a brief essay entitled *Discuss the advantages and disadvantages of public transport*. Write four or five paragraphs, using some of the vocabulary that you have studied in this unit.

Suggestions:

- Introduce the topic and explain to the reader how you will approach the essay.
- **Identify** the examples of public transport which you are going to discuss.
- Indicate the **criteria** by which you will judge their advantages and disadvantages.
- **Analyse** these advantages and disadvantages.
- Bring your writing to a conclusion or summarise what you have said (see Unit 6).

_____

_____

_____

_____

_____

_____

_____

_____

_____

_____

_____

_____

_____

_____

Expressing opinions tentatively

May, possible, unlikely, probably

In academic writing you will often need to express ideas and findings tentatively, indicating that they are not absolutely certain, or perhaps doubtful.

There are many ways to avoid making definite statements. The words **may**, **possible**, **unlikely** and **probably**, which we consider in this unit, are useful.

The sample texts on this page show you how professional writers use these terms. (Don't worry if there are words and ideas here that you don't understand – just concentrate on the use and meaning of the key words.)

When you have looked through the sample texts, work through the exercises to consolidate your understanding of how to use these terms.

It is not known, and will **probably** never be known, when he began writing poetry. The answer **almost certainly** lay in the sack of papers that Susan Owen, on her son's strict instructions, burnt at his death (Stallworthy 1977).

A fish who swims obliquely behind another fish **may** gain a hydrodynamic advantage from the turbulence produced by the fish in front. This **could** be partly why fish school. A related trick concerned with air turbulence is known to racing cyclists, and it **may** account fot the v-formation of flying birds. There is **probably** competition to avoid the disadvantageous position at the head of the flock. **Possibly** the birds take turns as unwilling leader (Dawkins 1985).

When interviewing Margaret, the therapist found her to be moderately depressed, but to an extent in keeping with her problems. He thought she had shown moderate suicidal intent in taking the overdose, particularly because she took it at night when **unlikely** to be discovered and repeated the act on waking in the morning. However, he also thought she **might** have been trying to demonstrate the extent of her distress to her family and **possibly** to her husband (Hawton and Catalan 1990).

At the end of treatment the therapist thought that Liz would **probably** experience further problems in the future and so discussed with her **possible** ways of dealing with new difficulties (Hawton and Catalan 1990).

Part 1: May

Study this concordance, underlining or highlighting the central group of words that stand alone, as has been done in the first example. Then answer the questions which follow. You may like to look at question 1 before you start. (Don't worry that these are cut-off sentences – just familiarise yourself with the key words.)

```
g the collision of purely gravitational waves. <p> It may also be observed that, with the positive s
ular when &and;formula. As in all other solutions, it may also be noted that there are non-scalar cu
evious ages would have died. Consequently, the doctor may appear to play the role of God, the giver
lter the state of the receiving cell. This alteration may be either excitatory or inhibitory: that i
 beyond the horizon would present no problems. <p> It may be noted, however, that is the signs of th
and <i> bn </i> are series of arbitrary constants. It may be noted, of course, that non-integer valu
ng the females and only the subordinates do badly, it may be that it is only younger females that fa
 are beginning to resolve because by then the patient may be more willing to consider, for example,
patient usually relate to the terminal illness, there may be times when they arise from some separat
 and the opening of the urethra. Following this there may be discomfort on urination, and a vicious
ut there was machinery to recruit volunteers. So this may be the sort of case we are looking for, a
ng with them properties such as drug resistance which may be of value to the host cell. Perhaps the
en convincingly confirmed. But, however suggestive it may be, the fact that a given phenomenon is su
           the game is likely to last. This assessment may become an important part of strategy. If I
  may be experienced differently in the contexts). It may even be possible for background, contextua
   and the answers are less conclusive. Generally, one may expect that, for a combination of gravitat
t has arranged for embryos to construct organisms. We may find unifying principles in patterns of ge
ssed hope in the coming of the Age of the Holy Spirit may have had its origin in the Jewish concept
   to do. Third, the duty is owed to institutions which may have authority but only towards other peop
 some cases bodies were covered with red ochre, which may have been intended to simulate blood, in t
cessary to do experiments on the embryo itself, which may involve opening chicken eggs and observing
he problem quickly occurs to any human. An individual may not be able to reach his own head, but not
s limited, and that one of the limitations is that it may not err much. For such a limitation defeat
the first site of infection is the cervix, when there may not be any local pain. Sometimes there is
ent problems but also to deal with some of those that may occur subsequently. However, there are spe
ial body may or may not actually be moving, so a mind may or may not actually be thinking. By 'thoug
s is not always attributable to 'poor motivation'. It may result from inconveniently timed appointme
ding has been employed. In addition, deep lacerations may result in disfiguring scars. The deformity
nse is made. <p> Studies of working memory in animals may seem to be rather remote from <pb n=160> t
nterested altruism! <p> Superficially, these theories may seem incompatible with the statement that
 in sexually transmitted diseases in Sandiago, but it may well take more than that to make any impre
 is free. Although the treatment is free, the patient may well be asked to pay for the tests used in
reasons, indeed in order that they should do so, they may well lead to different outcomes on particu
```

1 Which of the following statements do you think are correct? Tick your answer in the box.

May can be used to indicate that something is possible but that it also might not be true   correct ☐   incorrect ☐

May is used with some verbs to suggest that the reader think about something   correct ☐   incorrect ☐

May indicates that something is probably not true   correct ☐   incorrect ☐

2 Which word can be used after **may** in order to show that something is more likely to be true than untrue?

may _____

3 Which *verbs* commonly follow the word **may**?

may _*appear*_____   may _____

may _____   may _____

may _____   may _____

may _____   may _____

may _____   may _____

4 Look at the concordance and list the phrases in which the use of **may** does not indicate that there is doubt, but rather that the writer wants to bring something to the reader's attention.

_____*it may also be observed that*_____   _____

_____

5 Which *pronoun* (*I, you, he, she, it, we, they*) is most often found before **may** in academic writing?

_____ may

6 Draw a line matching each part of a sentence on the left hand side with its corresponding part on the right. (Note: This is an extension exercise, not necessarily related to the concordance given.)

Consequently, the doctor may appear to play	may be of value to the host cell.
It is often better to leave such exploration until the patient's difficulties are beginning to resolve because by then	have been intended to simulate blood, in the hope of averting physical extinction.
Plasmids are often symbionts rather than parasites: that is, they benefit rather than injure their hosts, for example by carrying with them properties such as drug resistance which	may well be asked to pay for the tests used in diagnosis.
In some cases, bodies were covered with red ochre, which may	from inconveniently timed appointments or travel difficulties.
An individual may not be able to reach	the role of God, the giver and taker of life.
Although, the treatment is free, the patient	his own head, but nothing is easier than for a friend to do it for him.
It may result	the patient may be more willing to consider, for example, that his act was based on hostile and manipulation motives.

CREATE

7 Now you can use the word **may** yourself. Rewrite the following sentences using **may** in order to make these statements tentative.

- In addition, deep lacerations result in disfiguring scars. The deformity or disfigurement is an added cause for depression and regret at having failed.

- In a proportion of cases the first site of infection is the cervix, where there is not any local pain.

- This alteration is either excitatory or inhibitory; that is, it makes the receiving cell more or less likely to emit impulses itself.

Part 2: Possible

Study this concordance, underlining or highlighting the central group of words that stand alone, as has been done in the first example. Then answer the questions which follow. You may like to look at question 1 before you start. (Remember – just familiarise yourself with the key words.)

Group 1

```
l change. They argue further that it should be possible to eliminate the long-term effect by a proce
he hearts of the majority of the people. It is possible for such sentiments of approval of this past
l result in you putting on fat. However, it is possible to lose weight and not suffer a lar
 overall this view is still widely held, it is possible to point to several cases of reversal when,
emember that progress in biology is often made possible by technical advances. In understanding brai
ogress in chemistry was just beginning to make possible the effective study of very large molecules
well as IV, are curved. Consequently it is not possible in general to analyse the singularity struct
nst the acceptance of authority vary it is not possible to discover in advance how strong the reason
he egg, effectively, has no nucleus. It is now possible to introduce another nucleus into this egg.
o not eat then – but it means that it is often possible to catch up on lost sleep by taking a nap at
 if they had any. Although it is theoretically possible for evolution to proceed in this direction,
 for setting up a trust were addressed, it was possible to conceive of the trust as inhering in cert
ations. From the scales engraved on it, it was possible to determine the positions of the so-called
r plains of aestheticism from where it becomes possible to adopt a universal outlook, a point of vie
```

Group 2

```
King, and in that of his closest adviser, as a possible solution to the economic crisis which many f
hose reasons. If they do not then deny them as possible bases for their own action they defeat the v
mainly by removing misunderstandings and a few possible objections. Implicitly the argument appeals
hatcherism as alien ideological territory. One possible means of reconciling the new right and Thatc
es where this would seem to have been the only possible method of transmission, but the extent of th
n certain cells than the normal virus, and the possible risks attached to such vaccines vastly outwe
```

Group 3

```
position to develop Reiter's disease and it is possible that the organism responsible for NGU can ac
an play little part in the effect, it is still possible that associative interference might be respo
```

1 Notice that the use of **possible** in the three groups of concordance examples differs slightly. Which meaning corresponds to the correct group? Tick your answer in the box.

	Group 1	Group 2	Group 3
To show that something is not definite	☐	☐	☐
To indicate an ability to do something	☐	☐	☐
To indicate that a statement/idea might be true	☐	☐	☐

2 For which group could you substitute *it may be* for *it is possible*?

Group 1 ☐   Group 2 ☐   Group 3 ☐

3 Write down the nouns that directly follow **possible** (the first has been done for you).

possible _solution_____   possible _____

possible _____   possible _____

possible _____   possible _____

4 Write down the *non-finite verbs* (preceded by *to*) that follow **possible.**

possible _to eliminate_____   possible _____

possible _____   possible _____

possible _____   possible _____

possible _____   possible _____

possible _____   possible _____

possible _____

5 List some phrases which use parts of the verbs **to be, to become** or **to make** directly before **possible**.

it should be possible   possible

_____ possible   possible

_____ possible   possible

_____ possible   possible

_____ possible   possible

_____ possible

6 In the following examples, fill the blank with the missing word. (Note: This is an extension exercise, not necessarily related to the concordances given.) Choose from the following lists:

verbs	*nouns*	*preposition*	*conjunction*
to point	risks	for	that
to lose	solution		
	means		

a The idea of a National Government, then, had implanted itself in the mind of the King, and in that of his closest adviser, as a **possible** _____ to the economic crisis which many felt to be imminent.

b It appears that certain people have a predisposition to develop Reiter's disease and it is **possible** _____ the organism responsible for NGU can act as a 'trigger' which sets off the inflammatory process.

c It is **possible** _____ weight and not suffer a large drop in metabolic rate.

d Although overall this view is still widely held, it is **possible** _____ to several cases of reversal when, for example, agriculturalists reverted to hunting and gathering.

e One **possible** _____ of reconciling the new right and Thatcherism to the Conservative tradition would be to abandon the emphasis on 'authority' and emphasise the duality of Conservative thought.

f It has been shown that inactivated herpes virus is more capable of inducing cancerous change in certain cells than the normal virus, and the **possible** _____ attached to such vaccines vastly outweigh any dubious advantages.

g Although it is theoretically **possible** _____ evolution to proceed in this direction, it seems to be only in the social insects that it has actually happened.

7 Decide whether to use **may** or **possible** in the following concordance lines.

```
overall this view is still widely held, it is _____ to point to several cases of reversal when,

ages would have died. Consequently, the doctor _____ appear to play the role of God, the giver

 inning to resolve because by then the patient _____ more willing to consider, for example,

 to do experiments on the embryo itself, which _____ involve opening chicken eggs and observing

emember that progress in biology is often made _____ by technical advances. In understanding brai

nst the acceptance of authority vary it is not _____ to discover in advance how strong the reason

s been employed. In addition, deep lacerations _____ result in disfiguring scars. The deformity

 if they had any. Although it is theoretically _____ for evolution to proceed in this direction,

r plains of aestheticism from where it becomes _____ to adopt a universal outlook, a point of vie

blems but also to deal with some of those that _____ occur subsequently. However, there are spe

 ses bodies were covered with red ochre, which _____ have been intended to simulate blood, in t

incingly confirmed. But, however suggestive it _____ be, the fact that a given phenomenon is su

King, and in that of his closest adviser, as a _____ solution to the economic crisis which many f

mainly by removing misunderstandings and a few _____ objections. Implicitly the argument appeals
```

8 Now you can use **possible** yourself. Rewrite these sentences, using **possible,** in order to make tentative rather than definite statements.

• Sentiments of approval of a violent past coexist with abhorrence for most current acts of violence.

_____

_____

• One means of reconciling the new right and Thatcherism to the conservative tradition would be to abandon the emphasis on 'authority' and emphasise the duality of Conservative thought.

_____

_____

_____

Part 3: Unlikely

Study this concordance, underlining or highlighting the central group of words that stand alone, as has been done in the first example. Then answer the questions which follow. You may like to look at question 1 before you start. (Remember – just familiarise yourself with the key words.)

```
lude one or two explanations which are clearly unlikely and which he can easily refute. Facili
forms of apparatus with layouts that seem very unlikely, as far as one can tell, to induce such stra
eement on inter-nationalisation was considered unlikely, Britain would also prepare to operate in a
he expiration of three years. If the extremely unlikely event transpires that in three years he has
as not changed since. The first alternative is unlikely. It is hard to see why a code in which GGC m
t law and practice, to a large extent, make it unlikely that property of any considerable value will
hich require development and evaluation. It is unlikely that any one method would suit all patients
iny of the testator's intention. It seems most unlikely that the testator had any intention of this
s always been in a state of flux, it is highly unlikely that this process will end at any particular
ited to late classical law, although it is not unlikely that the same applied earlier. <p> To conclu
ht take up to one hour. This not only makes it unlikely that employers will allow many such sessions
 add 2 lb (1 kg) of fat in one day. It is most unlikely that you would do this! <p> However, you mig
 to buy a reasonably large diary. It is highly unlikely that you will be doing this around January b
ends of slowing production. Moreover, it seems unlikely that herds in developing countries can long
d, sexual partner. It is also possible, though unlikely, that the prolonged course of treatment was
      he female. Although it might seem highly unlikely, there are considerable similarities between
life, to be an interesting business, but it is unlikely to cause Chattertonís reputation to inch bac
 genes for jumping high and ostentatiously are unlikely to be eaten by predators because predators t
her cases this is not so. Teaching at night is unlikely to prove popular (with teacher or pupil!) an
arsh tits, or willow tits (to be fair, you are unlikely to be able to distinguish the latter two unl
ternational authority). As this was considered unlikely to succeed because, of US opposition, a Euro
 <p> Once the code is established, then, it is unlikely to change. Its universality is to be expecte
thern-led leadership, it could be presumed, is unlikely to succeed – indeed, in certain circumstance
ect of its loss when the context is changed is unlikely to match exactly the reduction suffered by t
 not one disease but many, and the answers are unlikely to be the same for all of them. <p> Many peo
d purines had to come from somewhere. Food was unlikely to provide exactly the right nucleic acids r
y, and thought are spent on the service, it is unlikely to improve. The standard textbook on the ven
 a complex one, subsidiary aspects of care are unlikely to be overlooked. Finally, the problem-orien
imself. Problems in personal relationships are unlikely to be altered directly by medication. Howeve
particularly because she took it at night when unlikely to be discovered and repeated the act on wak
e common for there to be a cervicitis. This is unlikely to produce anything more than a slight incre
et, a grubby towel under his arm, he looked an unlikely trainer, nothing like the smooth Mr Plumpton
 most of the problem is due to prostitutes (an unlikely truth in any European country), the examinin
```

FAMILIARISE

1 When do you think you would use the word **unlikely**? Tick your answer in the box.

To indicate that something is impossible	correct ☐	incorrect ☐
To indicate that something is possible but doubtful	correct ☐	incorrect ☐
To indicate that you do not like something	correct ☐	incorrect ☐

2 List some *adverbs* that are commonly used before **unlikely** in order to show how doubtful the writer is about something.

_____*clearly*___ unlikely   _____ unlikely   _____ unlikely

_____ unlikely   _____ unlikely   _____ unlikely

3 List some *verbs* that are commonly used before and directly after **unlikely.**

_____*seem*___ unlikely   unlikely _____*to cause*_____   unlikely _____

_____ unlikely   unlikely _____   unlikely _____

_____ unlikely   unlikely _____   unlikely _____

_____ unlikely   unlikely _____   unlikely _____

_____ unlikely   unlikely _____   unlikely _____

_____ unlikely   unlikely _____   unlikely _____

                              unlikely _____   unlikely _____

4 Which words are most commonly used after **unlikely**?

unlikely _____   unlikely _____

5 Can you write down examples of **unlikely** used as an *adjective* to describe a thing or a person?

unlikely *event* _____   unlikely _____   unlikely _____

6 Draw a line matching each part of a sentence on the left hand side with its corresponding part on the right. (Note: The following are extension exercises, not necessarily related to the concordance.)

As regards property, it should be noticed that law and practice, to a large extent, make it unlikely	can long continue to expand, given the already serious problems from overgrazing and desertification.
It seems unlikely that herds in developing countries	are unlikely to be the same for all of them.
If society in all its aspects has always been in a state of flux, it is	and the night shift in a hospital ward cannot be made equivalent to the day shift (except in intensive care units which are continuously busy).
Although the symptoms displayed by the patient usually relate to terminal illness, there may be times when	to catch up on lost sleep by taking a nap at this time.
It is possible to point	they arise from some separate, independent condition.
Cancer is not one disease but many, and the answers	when unlikely to be discovered and repeated the act on waking in the morning.
He thought she had shown moderate suicidal intent in taking the overdose, particularly because she took it at night	highly unlikely that this process will end at any particular time.
Teaching at night is unlikely to prove popular (with teacher or pupil)	that property of any considerable value will come into the direct ownership of an infant.
It is often possible	to several cases of reversal.

7 Decide which of the words you have studied so far in this unit (**may, possible** or **unlikely**) should be used in the following sentences.

a Although it is theoretically _____ for evolution to proceed in this direction, it seems to be only in the social insects that it has actually happened.

b Although the treatment is free, the patient _____ be asked to pay for the tests used in diagnosis.

c As regards property, it should be noticed that law and practice, to a large extent, make it _____ that property of any considerable value will come into the direct ownership of an infant.

d His fervently expressed hope in the coming of the Age of the Holy Spirit _____ have had its origin in the Jewish concept of the Messianic Age.

e Although this book is about ideas rather than techniques, it is important to remember that progress in biology is often made _____ by technical advances.

f If society in all its aspects has always been in a state of flux, it is highly _____ that this process will end at any particular time.

g If the extremely _____ event transpires that in three years he has discovered nothing of his partner's past, then why should he complain?

h In some cases bodies were covered with red ochre, which _____ have been intended to simulate blood.

i It is also possible, though _____ , that the prolonged course of treatment was inadequate to eliminate the organism responsible.

j It seems _____ that herds in developing countries can long continue to expand, given the already serious problems from over-grazing and desertification.

8 Now you can use **unlikely** yourself. Look at the following information and then write a sentence using **unlikely** to indicate tentatively whether or not a single method of supplying a particular drug would suit all patients.

- This drug can be taken orally, via skin patches (which require regular changing) or via an implant.
- Some patients react negatively to the tablet form of the drug or forget to take it regularly.
- The implant involves minor surgery and can cause temporary discomfort.
- Some patients dislike skin patches for aesthetic reasons.

_____

_____

_____

_____

_____

Part 4: Probably

Study this concordance, underlining or highlighting the central group of words that stand alone, as has been done in the first example. Then answer the questions which follow. You may like to look at question 1 before you start. (Remember – just familiarise yourself with the key words.)

```
  of other bacteria-negative causes. It is probably a mistake to regard the urethral syndrome as one
rations to specify each base. Since it is  probably an exaggeration to suppose that as much as 50 per
silver top milk. The lunchtime meal will   probably be fairly high in fat (such as a pasty or pie; or
of the risk is hard to quantify. It would  probably be true to say, however, that the long and passio
cance of our social organisation. This is  probably because they are all adapted to forest or woodlan
 active person must be considered as most  probably being due to a sexually transmitted disease. That
the patient has coped previously. This is  probably best accomplished by asking the patient to descri
 at an early stage of Chinese history. It  probably came there from Babylonia, where the simplest for
 his nose, and came up with a shriek that  probably carried as far as the bridge party two streets aw
nd predictable. The resulting competition  probably causes the animals to occupy small but adequate t
hen he became a professor, his reputation  probably depended largely on his studies of the capillary
 though this involves sharing food. It is  probably for similar reasons that some spiders cooperate i
s. And despite his kinship with Degas, he  probably had more immediate precedents for his renditions
reness' and goes on to say that awareness  probably has survival value because it enables animals to
fferent, at least in terms of degree, and  probably in relation to the extent to which the riots were
y defined, not merely medical care, it is  probably inevitable in our present society that resources
wn way of interpreting Darwin's ideas. He  probably learned them not from Darwin's own writings, but
6> now the other. The truth of the matter  probably lies somewhere in between. As Miller argues, ther
xperienced in at least 100 000 years, and  probably much longer. Stephen Schneider, George Woodwell,
th injury problems in later life and will  probably never enjoy the relative prosperity of their firs
ansposons are relatively simple, they are  probably not primitive, because they can replicate only in
es this weight off in a month or two will  probably not be successful in the long term. Unless the di
t'. The invention of the mechanical clock  probably occurred after 1277, since if it had occurred ear
ons were established. The orang-utan thus  probably reached its definitive form by evolution from a r
rmanent characteristics such as race and,  probably, religion may be taken into account, but transien
to help the patient change his attitudes.  Probably the most effective means is to find a task which
es without bringing back the crowds. Most  probably the solution in the longer term will be a switch
p the extinction of the suckers and, very  probably, the extinction of the whole population too. <p>
ext to the Beatles and Mick Jagger he was  probably the best-known teenage 'pin up'. The footballer a
l principles of political morality. It is  probably true to say that no political cause, no one visio
rgy in education was being attacked, and,  probably wrongly, that the reform of the faults of the pre
```

1 Which of the following statements do you think are correct? Tick your answer in the box.

Probably is used to indicate that the statement being made
is more likely to be true than untrue   correct ☐ incorrect ☐

Probably indicates that a statement is as likely to be true as untrue   correct ☐ incorrect ☐

Probably indicates that a statement is likely to be untrue   correct ☐ incorrect ☐

2 Which words can be used before **probably** in order to make the statement seem almost certain?

_____ probably   _____ probably

3 Which words can be used after **probably** in order to indicate negativity (that something is almost certain to be untrue)?

probably _____   probably _____

4 Judging from the concordance, what is the subject (e.g. *I*, *you*, *he*, *it*, *the book*) most commonly used with **probably**?

_____

5 In the following examples, choose the appropriate word to fill the blank spaces. (Note: The following are extension exercises, not necessarily related to the concordance given.) Choose from the following lists:

conjunction	non-finite verb	finite verb
that	to lose	came
	to prove	reflected
	to be altered	depended
	to discover	become
		occurred

a You could **probably** _____ far more healthy by the simple expedient of 'going back in time' in terms of some of your daily activity.

b It appears that certain people have a predisposition to develop Reiter's disease and it is **possible** _____ the organism responsible for NGU can act as a 'trigger' which sets off the inflammatory process.

c It **probably** _____ there from Babylonia, where the simplest form of the outflow type had already been in use before the time of the early Shang period (c. 1500 BC).

d As regards property, it should be noticed that law and practice, to a large extent, make it **unlikely** _____ property of any considerable value will come into the direct ownership of an infant.

e Problems in personal relationships are **unlikely** _____ directly by medication.

f Van Gogh's letter of June 1988 **probably** _____ his own experiences of his last months in Paris, during the early winter of 1887–88.

g It is **possible** _____ weight and not suffer a large drop in metabolic rate.

h It is **unlikely** _____ any one method would suit all patients and therefore it is best to discuss with the patient alternative approaches to find out which seems the most likely to succeed.

i The invention of the mechanical clock **probably**_____ after 1277.

j Because the reasons against the acceptance of authority vary it is not **possible** _____ in advance how strong the reasons for acceptance of the authority need be to be sufficient.

k At the time when he became professor, his reputation **probably** _____ largely on his studies of the capillary circulation and of the blood cells concerned with defence against bacterial invasion.

l Teaching at night is **unlikely** _____ popular (with teacher or pupil!) and the night shift in a hospital ward cannot be made equivalent to the day shift (except for intensive care units which are continuously busy).

6 In each group of concordances below, one of the words you have studied in this unit is missing. Decide which word is needed for each group and write it in.

Group 1

```
to one hour. This not only makes it          that employers will allow many such sessions
owing production. Moreover, it seems          that herds in developing countries can long
loss when the context is changed is           to match exactly the reduction suffered by t
blems in personal relationships are           to be altered directly by medication. Howeve
y because she took it at night when           to be discovered and repeated the act on wak
```

Group 2

```
e risk is hard to quantify. It would          be true to say, however, that the long and
d. Their society may have, and most           has, changed radically and often since the
a methods of management; success is           most likely where both are utilised. The us
ury problems in later life and will           never enjoy the relative prosperity of thei
where he learned Arabic. Later he             visited Spain. His outstanding role in the
```

Group 3

```
the receiving cell. This alteration           be either excitatory or inhibitory: that i
izon would present no problems. It            be noted, however, that if the signs of th
late to the terminal illness, there           be times when they arise from some separat
riments on the embryo itself, which           involve opening chicken eggs and observing
occurs to any human. An individual            not be able to reach his own head, but not
```

Group 4

```
They argue further that it should be          to eliminate the long-term effect by a proce
n – but it means that it is often             to catch up on lost sleep by taking a nap at
cells than the normal virus, and the          risks attached to such vaccines vastly outwe
om the scales engraved on it, it was          to determine the positions of the so-called
erapist. This person should whenever          be the one who takes responsibility for coun
```

7 Underline examples of use of tentative language in the following text.

Ramapithecus was one of several primates, such as the baboons, which came down from the trees to develop terrestrial living. Its dental adaptations to hard savannah fruits and seeds probably preceded the development of bipedalism, which may itself have been originally connected with foraging, reaching upward to browse on bushes for example. *Ramapithecus* lasted for about seven million years and may have then given rise to the first true hominid, *Australopithecus,* which has a similar dental structure. *Ramapithecus* may not have been carnivorous, and the association between hunting, travel, and bipedalism probably emerged only with the true hominids. (Cook 1985)

8 Consider the underlined words in the following passages and then group them (in the columns that follow) to indicate which show that the writer is **very sure** about the truth of the information being given, when the writer is **fairly sure** that the statement is true, when the writer is **not very sure** and when the writer is **very doubtful** about the truth of a statement.

It is <u>often possible</u> to catch up on lost sleep by taking a nap at this time.

Severe shortage of vitamins and minerals is rare. However, any diet high in foods that contain few vitamins and minerals is <u>likely</u> to lead to some degree of illness.

It is also <u>possible, though unlikely</u>, that the prolonged course of treatment was inadequate to eliminate the organism responsible.

It seems <u>probable</u> that some doctors carry out mercy killings by administering large doses of pain-killing drugs which shorten life significantly, and the law <u>may well</u> protect them from liability. However, such trust is not shown towards relatives and friends who assist suffering people in this way: they <u>must</u> run the gauntlet of a legal process which accords no formal recognition to the circumstances under which they killed.

If the <u>extremely unlikely</u> event transpires that in three years he has discovered nothing of his partner's past, then why should he complain?

These three deforestation factors <u>could well</u> eliminate a total of at least 200 000 sq km of forest during the 1990s.

The invention of the mechanical clock <u>probably</u> occurred after 1277, since if it had occurred earlier it is <u>almost certain</u> that it would have been included in Volume IV of the *Libros del saber de astronomica*.

2000 calories-worth of meals in a day would need to be supplemented by fourteen cakes at 500 calories each, or around twenty bars of chocolate, to add 2 lb (1 kg) of fat in one day. It is <u>most unlikely</u> that you would do this!

It <u>seems unlikely</u> that herds in developing countries can long continue to expand, given the already serious problems from over-grazing and desertification.

Consequently it is <u>not possible in general</u> to analyse the singularity structure in such detail.

There are several different causes of such symptoms in the male, but the development of either symptom in a sexually active person must be considered as <u>most probably</u> being due to a sexually transmitted disease.

They argue further that it <u>should be possible</u> to eliminate the long-term effect by a procedure designed to extinguish a context.

Very sure

Not very sure

_____

_____

_____

_____

_____

_____

Fairly sure

Very doubtful

_____

_____

_____

_____

_____

_____

_____

_____

_____

_____

9 Now you can use these words yourself.

The following graph shows the results of a informal small-scale study carried out in Australia in 1995. Since the study was not large scale and the researcher did not claim that the sample was necessarily representative of the whole population, the implications of the results must be written up tentatively. Look carefully at the table and then write a brief report on these results in the Australian context, entitled *Ownership of Computers and Modems in the Australian Home*.

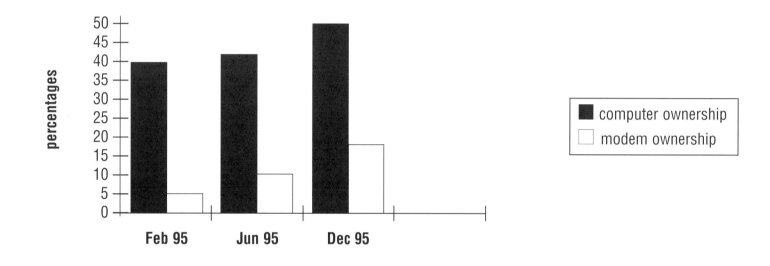

_____

_____

_____

_____

_____

_____

Drawing conclusions and summarising

Paragraphs concluding a section of writing

In **conclusion**, it seems that we cannot accept without question the dramatic increase in recorded crime as corresponding to a real increase in victimisation of the same proportions. But it would be wishful thinking to explain away all, or even most, of the increase as an artefact of recording changes. We can plausibly infer that crime has been increasing in the last two to three decades, presenting a problem for explanation and policy (McGregor and Pimlott 1991).

The picture which has emerged in this chapter is, perhaps inevitably, a confused one. It would be still more so if all the ways in which nucleic acid molecules can recombine had been included. It may help if I **summarise** the main **conclusions**. On the one hand, nucleic acids arise only as copies of pre-existing nucleic acids. In this sense, genetic information is potentially immortal. On the other hand, pieces of DNA are continually being separated and brought together in new combinations. In higher organisms the common process of recombination is the sexual one, and to that extent is confined to the DNA of a single species (Smith 1989).

Thus, a whole range of decisions would not be left merely to the instinct of the doctor, good though he or she may be, but would be set down in a form which is at the same time authoritative, yet flexible and able to change if circumstances demand. For we must never lose sight of the fact that the issues involved are moral ones; and that though doctors may be experts in medicine, they are no more competent or qualified to speak on moral issues than you or I (Kennedy 1988).

Concluding, summarising

When drawing a conclusion from a section of your writing or when bringing your essay to its final statement, you may find it helpful to use terms which indicate that you are **concluding** or **summarising**.

In this unit, we will look at words related to these two functions as well as the terms **thus** and **it is clear** which can also indicate to the reader that you are drawing a conclusion.

Conclusions can occur as final paragraphs or as final sentences within a paragraph.

The sample texts on this page show you how professional writers use these terms. (Don't worry if there are words and ideas here that you don't understand – just concentrate on the use and meaning of the key words.)

When you have looked through the sample texts, work through the exercises to consolidate your understanding of how to use these terms.

Some final sentences which summarise the content of a paragraph

Whatever the details it seems **clear that**: (1) except in the case of India, little of the capital flows took the form of a run down of sterling balances; (2) most of the investment flow was to the 'white Commonwealth', especially South Africa; and (3) the colonies saw net disinvestment (*20th Century British History*, Vol 2 No 1, OUP 1991).

Thus, in **summary**, the first duty of a doctor is to listen to and respect the wishes of his patient (Kennedy 1988).

Part 1: Concluding

Study this concordance, underlining or highlighting the central group of words that stand alone, as has been done in the first example. Then answer the questions which follow. You may like to look at question 1 before you start. (Don't worry that these are cut-off sentences – just familiarise yourself with the key words.)

Group 1

1. State will appear. For the time being let me **conclude** by admitting that the considerations adumbrat
2. recent history. But it would be simplistic to **conclude** either that the grave dangers forecast by the
3. ace-time can be extended. It is reasonable to **conclude** from this that, although there are colliding
4. remain unresolved for the time being. We can **conclude** only that unequivocal evidence for the existe
5. lier Pascal. It is not unreasonable, then, to **conclude** that the Beaux-Arts scheme at Penn was authen
6. he present two state units. One can therefore **conclude** that there is a sense of unity throughout the
7. the new response to the test stimuli, we may **conclude** that the stimulus used in acquisition and tha
8. e the authority of this law. We are forced to **conclude** that while the main argument does confer qual
9. perturbations. It is therefore reasonable to **conclude** that the existence of space-like singularitie
10. la. These will be described later. <p> We may **conclude** that, in all cases, the opposing waves mutual
11. et flavour showed no such preference. We must **conclude** then that, at the very least, a conditioned i
12. (that is, to what part of the brain). <p> To **conclude** this chapter, I would like to return to the p
13. e to grief. Objections. I will **conclude** this chapter by considering a few objections
14. will be irrelevant. It would be premature to **conclude**, however, that the transfer seen in such an e
15. are to understand how we perceive things. To **conclude**, I will list what these questions are, and re
16. just government of foreign countries. We must **conclude**, therefore, that the duty to support just ins
17. tances of trusts in the papyri at all. <p> To **conclude**. The evidence for the use of trust clauses is
18. nlikely that the same applied earlier. <p> To **conclude**. The texts of Roman law bring us to the intri

Group 2

19. cuniary dispositions. <p> From this it can be **concluded** first that Aristo interprets the disposition
20. onditions (7.3) are satisfied. <p> It must be **concluded** that the above solution cannot be interprete
21. ains terms of the form (7.10). It may thus be **concluded** that, if the leading terms in the expansions

Group 3

22. is the argument of Part Four. Our provisional **conclusion** can be no more than that Rawls and others a
23. ion experiments. <p> Evidence to support this **conclusion** comes from a further set of studies by Hone
24. conditioning. One advantage of accepting this **conclusion** is that it provides, with its assumption th
25.   uences of the required length. This **conclusion** is supported by the fact that changes in th
26. er considerations. <p> Theoretically the main **conclusion** of the foregoing discussion is in the empha
27. of the initial approaching waves. <p> At the **conclusion** of this section, it may be noted that Ferra
28. on, 1988). It is perhaps too early to reach a **conclusion** on this point, but a repeat of the period o
29. problem. <p> The above arguments lead to the **conclusion** that the usual initial data for colliding p
30. trial of the test. This result encourages the **conclusion** that appropriate contextual cues must be pr
31. ming but it is enough to prompt the tentative **conclusion** that, in addition to the habituation proces
32. zi Movement. In fact, much points towards the **conclusion** that, despite its centrality to Hitler's ow
33. rid theory is likely to result. <p> The chief **conclusion** to emerge from the work discussed in this c
34. to validate a testatorís intentions. The main **conclusion** which this section and the preceding one al
35. ted as showing the direction of crime. <p> In **conclusion,** it seems that we cannot accept without que
36. ee how it could be otherwise. <p> The natural **conclusion,** then, is that the basic body plans of the
37. kind of person. I feel there can be only one **conclusion.** If ethnologists are truly interested in an
38. of which he has spent all his life. <p> These **conclusions** appear paradoxical. Ought not the pharmaco
39.   interpreted. In this chapter so far certain **conclusions** have been reached about the similarities a
40. included. It may help if I summarise the main **conclusions.** On the one hand, nucleic acids arise only

1 As you look through the examples in the concordances, you may notice that some of these **conclusions** are tentative and others are very definite. Write down the numbers of the concordances that are:

particularly tentative _____

particularly definite _____

2 Look at the concordance examples. Write down the way three writers have indicated that the information at present available is not adequate for a particular conclusion.

_____

_____

_____

3 Write down the way three writers of the examples in the concordances have indicated that they are absolutely sure of their conclusions.

_____

_____

_____

4 Write down the way three writers have indicated that they think their conclusions are acceptable.

_____

_____

_____

5 Write down the way two writers have indicated that they are aware that the conclusions they are drawing may later be proved to be wrong or incomplete (i.e. that they are drawing tentative conclusions).

_____

_____

6 Which words are used to indicate that the previous argument or information leads to the conclusion?

_____   _____   _____

7 List some adjectives that commonly precede the word **conclusion(s)**.

_____provisional_ conclusion   _____ conclusion

_____ conclusion   _____ conclusion

_____ conclusion   _____ conclusions

8 Note how the adjectives you have listed above qualify the conclusion in various ways, making it more or less definite, for example. Which adjectives indicate that the conclusion is not very definite?

_____   _____

9 Which of the following statements do you think are correct? Tick your answer in the box.

A **conclusion** must make a definite statement	correct ☐	incorrect ☐
A **conclusion** often expresses an opinion based on information that has gone before	correct ☐	incorrect ☐
A **conclusion** always refers to information that has been presented beforehand	correct ☐	incorrect ☐
A **conclusion** can appear at the end of a paragraph	correct ☐	incorrect ☐
A **conclusion** only appears at the end of a chapter or essay	correct ☐	incorrect ☐

PRACTISE

10 In the following examples, fill the blanks with one of the following words: **conclude, concluded, conclusion, conclusions**. (Note: This is an extension exercise, not necessarily related to the concordances given.)

a It is perhaps too early to reach a _____ on this point, but a repeat of the period of inaction between 1982 and 1985 seems to be evident, within the current political context.

b It is not unreasonable, then, to _____ that the Beaux-Arts scheme at Penn was authentic.

c In this chapter so far certain _____ have been reached about the similarities and differences between trusts and legacies, and about the roles played by wording and by intention in the interpretation of trusts.

d We must _____ then that, at the very least, a conditioned inhibitor is a stimulus having motivational properties that a latent inhibitor lacks.

e From this it can be _____ first that Aristo interprets the dispositions as trusts.

f The force of the argument just presented may not be overwhelming but it is enough to prompt the tentative _____ that, in addition to the habituation process invoked by exposure to a stimulus, some other process comes into play and is responsible for latent inhibition.

11 The following paragraph is complete except for its final sentence. Write one sentence to conclude the paragraph, using one of the terms you have studied in this unit. Your conclusion will bring the reader's attention to an underlying cause of deforestation in tropical countries.

Many tropical countries suffer from poverty and overpopulation. These problems have led governments to exploit their natural forests in an attempt to alleviate both poverty and overpopulation. Because of this, massive numbers of trees have been logged and sold to foreign countries, workers from overpopulated urban areas have been encouraged to migrate to unpopulated forest areas where employment has become available and agriculture has been promoted on the cleared land, preventing possibilities of forest regrowth. _____

_____

_____

_____

_____

12 You have been asked to write an essay entitled *Discuss the effects of television violence on children*. Having researched the topic, you have written an essay based on the following framework.

Section 1: Introduction.

Section 2: Evidence of strong opinions among parents and teachers that television violence promotes antisocial behaviour in children.
- Parents report more aggressive behaviour during and after viewing violent television.
- Teachers report more antisocial behaviour among children whose television viewing is not controlled by parents.
- Evidence of reduced concentration among children who watch television for more than a certain time.

Section 3: The controversy between sociologists and psychologists on whether or not television violence has negative effects on children.
- Studies by sociologists tend to claim that there is not sufficient strong evidence that the viewing of violent television has negative effects on children.

- Studies by psychologists tend to claim that television viewing does affect the behaviour of children.
- Some sociologists who have conducted studies in this area are employed by television companies.

Section 4: Lack of convincing empirical evidence that television violence promotes antisocial behaviour in children.
- Studies which show effects show only very slight effects.
- Some studies show no effect.

Section 5: Some evidence that watching violence in news programs may promote children's awareness of the actual level of violence in their own neighbourhoods.
- A study in a war-torn region indicates that children who watch the news have more realistic perception of the extent of violence in their own surroundings.

Section 6: Conclusion.

Now write that final section, the concluding paragraph.

_____

_____

_____

_____

_____

_____

_____

_____

_____

Part 2: Summarising

Study these concordances, underlining or highlighting the central group of words that stand alone, as has been done in the first example. Then answer the questions which follow. You may like to look at question 1 before you start.
(Remember – just familiarise yourself with the key words.)

Group 1

```
bine had been included. It may help if I summarise the main conclusions. On the one hand, nucleic ac
tion of the other. <p> I will now try to summarise what I have said about how an animal finds its wa
te supplies of vitamins and minerals. To summarise our suggestions for good nutrition: <p> •
le that the enzyme can recognise. <p> To summarise, the organic compounds found in cells are built u
eeling of what it was like. If I were to summarise, I would merely say we developed a capacity to pu
reatment were discussed in Chapter 4. To summarise, broadly speaking there are three main categories
irrelevant factors at this stage. <p> To summarise: the existing English law classifies as murder th
```

Group 2

```
ollowed by no significant event). <p> In summary, then, the basic facts of context-specificity in la
o achieve in the middle of the night. In summary, exercise is most efficient in the late afternoon.
therwise concerned in the case. Thus, in summary, the first duty of a doctor is to listen to and res
of the rhythms are likely to be less. In summary, with their development in infancy as well as their
```

1 Are the following statements correct? Tick your answer in the box.

In summary can be substituted by **to summarise**   correct ☐   incorrect ☐

When **to summarise** is attached to a subject (eg I)
it cannot be substituted by **in summary**   correct ☐   incorrect ☐

2 Write six different ways the writers of the above examples have used to indicate that they are about to summarise information that they have just provided.

_____

_____

_____

_____

_____

_____

3 Which words in the concordance examples are used to indicate that you have written your summary as a result of having considered previously stated information?

_____   _____

4 Look at the concordances and then at the following two paragraphs. Then answer the questions which follow.

> I will now try to **summarise** what I have said about how an animal finds its way about. Suppose it wants to go from A to a point E that it cannot see. There are two ways of achieving this. One is to follow a set of rules – an algorithm – such as 'go to B, then to D, and then to E'. The other is to build up a cognitive map of the region to be traversed. There is no doubt that the former method is often used. The relevant algorithms can be learnt by operant conditioning, as proposed by the behaviourists. There are, however, cases which are hard to explain in this way; examples are the ability of a rat to find a submerged support, and of a goby to leap to a pool it cannot see. These cases suggest that animals can form cognitive maps. However, this leaves much unexplained: how is the map formed, and how is it used? (Smith 1989)

> To **summarise** our suggestions for good nutrition:
> - At each meal choose a mix of proteins from animal and plant sources; have low-fat protein sources more frequently;
> - Carbohydrates should be in a 'natural', relatively unprocessed form, such as wholemeal bread, brown pasta and brown rice, roast potatoes. Avoid refined sugar, whether white or brown;
> - Have a piece of fruit with the meal;
> - Keep fat to a minimum; choose polyunsaturated rather than saturated fat (Ashcroft 1989).

Which of the following statements do you think are correct? Tick your answers in the box.

A **summary** gives the writer a chance to state his or her own opinion	correct ☐	incorrect ☐
A **summary** provides previously presented information in a tighter, briefer form	correct ☐	incorrect ☐
A **summary** is a brief statement of what has come before whereas a conclusion is a thoughtful reflection on what has come before	correct ☐	incorrect ☐
A **summary** is often a tentative statement	correct ☐	incorrect ☐

PRACTISE

5 The following statements are either **conclusions** or **summaries**. Indicate which you think they are by using the words **conclude** or **summarise**.

a We are forced to _____ that while the main argument does confer qualified and partial authority on just governments it invariably fails to justify the claims to authority which these governments make for themselves.

b To _____, broadly speaking there are three main categories of such patients [3 categories listed].

c It would be premature to _____, however, that the transfer seen in such an experiment depends on the acquisition of distinctiveness by the critical cues as a consequence of phase-one discrimination training.

d It may help if I _____ the main conclusions.

e It is therefore reasonable to _____ that the existence of space-like singularities is likely to be a generic feature of colliding plane wave solutions.

CREATE

6 Now that you have studied **conclusions** and **summaries**, write one paragraph in which you summarise the main differences between the two terms.

_____

_____

_____

_____

_____

_____

_____

7 Study the following graph, then summarise its findings in writing.

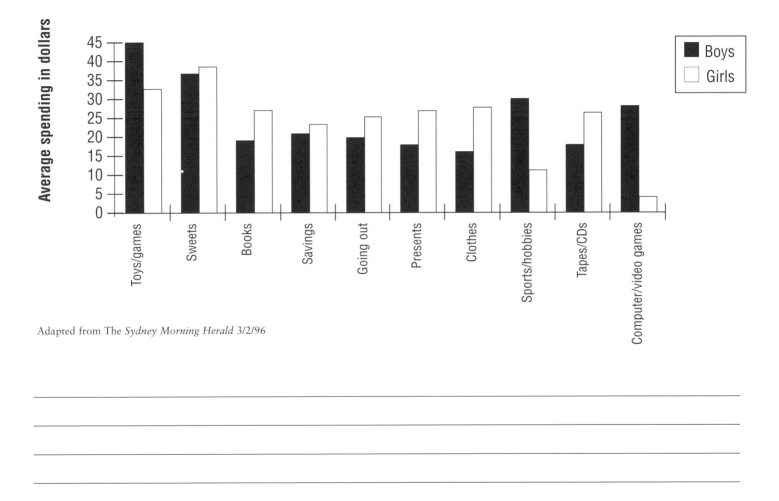

Spending by Australian children

Average spending in dollars

Categories: Toys/games, Sweets, Books, Savings, Going out, Presents, Clothes, Sports/hobbies, Tapes/CDs, Computer/video games

Legend: Boys, Girls

Adapted from The *Sydney Morning Herald* 3/2/96

Part 3: Clear that, thus

In the following sentences you will see how the expressions **(it is) clear that** and **thus** are used to mark final statements. Read them and answer the questions which follow. You may like to look at question 1 before you start.

Group 1

From these expressions it is **clear that**, for specific choices of initial data, the curvature singularity formed by the interacting waves degenerates to a coordinate singularity.

The table makes it **clear that** the bulk of overseas government expenditure was incurred within the rest of the sterling area(RSA), and did not therefore add directly to the dollar problem.

The concept is not a difficult one, for the last two sections have made it **clear that** what really mattered in setting up a trust was not the use of specific words, but the use of words or deeds which plainly expressed an intention to bind a trustee under a trust.

It should now be very **clear that** development is a dynamic process in which cells repeatedly interact with each other, change shape and position, and become different.

Whatever the details it seems **clear that**: (1) except in the case of India, little of the capital flows took the form of a run down of sterling balances; (2) most of the investment flow was to the 'white Commonwealth', especially South Africa; and (3) the colonies saw net disinvestment.

Group 2

Efficiency in competition is **thus** a prime source of selection and occurs in many aspects of social life.

It has **thus** been argued that the general structure of all colliding plane wave solutions is as illustrated in Figure 8.6.

Thus there has been more than enough time for selection to generate specific DNA sequences of the required length.

1 Which of the following statements do you think are correct? Tick your answer in the box.

(**It is**) **clear that** is used to indicate that you are sure of your final statement   correct ☐   incorrect ☐

Thus is used to indicate that you are not very sure of your final statement   correct ☐   incorrect ☐

Thus is used to indicate that previous information or argument has led
to your statement   correct ☐   incorrect ☐

(**It is**) **clear that** can be used to introduce either a summary or a conclusion   correct ☐   incorrect ☐

Thus never has the same function as **for this reason**   correct ☐   incorrect ☐

Thus links a cause with an effect   correct ☐   incorrect ☐

PRACTISE

2 Decide whether the missing word or word group in these sentences is **conclusion(s)**, **summarise**, **(it is) clear that** or **thus**. (Note: These are extension exercises, not necessarily related to the concordances you have studied.)

a Even if Dail members had thought otherwise, it must by now be _____ the ethos of the Irish Republic was still one in which it was impolitic to be in conflict with the church.

b It is perhaps too early to reach a _____ on this point, but a repeat of the period of inaction between 1982 and 1985 seems to be evident, within the current political context.

c The force of the argument just presented may not be overwhelming but it is enough to prompt the tentative _____ that, in addition to the habituation process invoked by exposure to a stimulus, some other process comes into play and is responsible for latent inhibition.

d It may _____ be concluded that, if the leading terms in the expansions for the functions f and g are given by (10.34), then the boundary conditions that are required for the solution to describe colliding plane are satisfied.

e It may help if I _____ the main _____ . On the one hand, nucleic acids arise only as copies of pre-existing nucleic acids. In this sense, genetic information is potentially immortal. On the other hand, pieces of DNA are continually being separated and brought together in new combinations.

f Given that macro-decisions inherently and inevitably condition micro-decisions, the principal focus of attention must be on the *political* decision-maker. _____ , it is _____ what we are in fact dealing with is an issue of political theory, the proper location of power and responsibility.

g In fact, much points towards the _____ that, despite its centrality to Hitler's own thinking, anti-Semitism was for the most part of no more than secondary importance as a factor shaping popular opinion in the Third Reich.

h To _____ , the organic compounds found in cells are built up and broken down by enzymes. These are protein molecules, which owe their specificity to their amino acid sequence, and hence ultimately to the genes.

i Finally, it is _____ centralised planning such as this must be kept under constant review, if it is to respond to changed needs and resources.

j In _____ , it seems that we cannot accept without question the dramatic increase in recorded crime as corresponding to a real increase in victimisation of the same proportions.

k Since the nucleus of a cell in the gut could give rise to a normal toad it is _____ no genetic information had been lost during the development of the gut, and the same holds for the skin nucleus. The important _____ is that all the cells in the body contain the same genetic information.

l This case provides an example of relatively poor use of brief treatment. It is _____ the therapist should have endeavoured at a much earlier stage to involve the parents in treatment, preferably by means of conjoint sessions with Pamela and her parents together.

m I will now try to _____ what I have said about how an animal finds its way about. Suppose it wants to go from A to a point E that it cannot see. There are two ways of achieving this. One is to follow a set of rules – an algorithm – such as 'go to B, then to D, and then to E'. The other is to build up a cognitive map of the region to be traversed. There is no doubt that the former method is often used. The relevant algorithms can be learnt by operant conditioning, as proposed by the behaviourists. There are, however, cases which are hard to explain in this way.

n It should now be very _____ development is a dynamic process in which cells repeatedly interact with each other, change shape and position, and become different.

o The natural _____ , then, is that the basic body plans of the different phyla represent structures which adapted some ancestral form to a particular way of life, and which have since been modified.

p _____ there has been more than enough time for selection to generate specific DNA sequences of the required length. This _____ is supported by the fact that changes in the fossil record, even rather rapid ones like the increase in human brain size in the last four million years, were slower by a factor of 1000 than the rate at which changes can be produced by artificial selection in laboratory populations or domestic animals.

3 In each of the concordance lists which follow, one of the words you have studied in this unit is missing. Decide which word is needed for each group.

f whatever political complexion. Finally, it is
res in schools, prisons, and to the army, but it is
lo did what he had to do to Desdemona. But it seems
clear transplantation and other experiments make it
from an aborted human embryo into the chick. It is
the *political* decision-maker. Thus, it is
f the industrialised societies. The report made it

}   {

centralised planning such as this must be kep
their efforts have little effect on the preva
this one bears the marks of defeat and despai
all nuclei contain the same genetic informati
this signal is the same in all higher vertebr
what we are in fact dealing with is an issue
adequate safeguards and standards were necess

---

ion of the new response to the test stimuli, we may
r must remain unresolved for the time being. We can
ively recent history. But it would be simplistic to
e target flavour showed no such preference. We must
come to less than one in 500. It is pretty safe to
nce and technology as commonplace', Noble and Price
if we are to understand how we perceive things. To

}   {

that the stimulus used in acquisition and tha
only that unequivocal evidence for the existe
either that the grave dangers forecast by the
then that, at the very least, a conditioned i
that the bats really were biased in favour of
, 'and we expect them and our architecture to be
, I will list what these questions are, and rem

---

mely complex process. However, here is a very brief
greed with the therapist that this was a reasonable
haps you did not know that you could shout <p> My
were provided in Chapter 4 (p. 75). In addition, a
cently, however, Kortlandt (1972), in an extesive
es (sizes) of the rhythms are likely to be less. In
difficult to achieve in the middle of the night. In

}   {

outlining the functions of food. <hd3> <i> Fo
of their difficulties. <hd3> Initial contract
does not convey the charm and intimacy with w
of those sections of the Act concerned with a
of palaeographical palaeoecological, and b
, with their development in infancy as well as
, exercise is most efficient in the late aftern

---

provided to the perceptual system. The organism is
se intending to specialise in dermatology. There is
nformation to produce responses to inputs. There is
nt feature. The problem of the origin of species is
transfer of latent inhibition would be incomplete.
ght be by parental design or due to natural events.
emory that enables us to recall events years later.

}   {

constantly cycling information and maintainin
quite a difference in the required training b
a valid distinction between body and mind. Mi
the problem of how such isolating mechanisms
the overshadowing effect can be explained wit
parents might decide to get the baby into a r
, although it might be useful to remember a par

4 Now you can use these words yourself. Use the following information to create your own conclusion to an argumentative essay entitled *Do you consider that the economic advantages of the cultivation of tobacco outweigh its disadvantages?* Try to use some of the expressions you have studied in this unit (**conclude, summarise, thus, it is clear that**).

Argument in favour

- Tobacco growing is suitable for small farmers.
- Most of the world's producers are small farmers.
- Many small businesses benefit from tobacco sales.
- Governments receive revenue from taxes on cigarettes.
- Demand for cigarettes tends to remain constant despite changes such as economic recession.
- Tobacco growing provides rural employment.

Argument against

- Tobacco consumption causes ill-health.
- Large government health-care costs for smoking-related illnesses.
- Production in other areas suffers from smoking-related illnesses
- Land used for tobacco production cannot be used for food production.
- Medicinal properties of plants found in forests

_____

_____

_____

_____

_____

Answers

Unit 1

Part 1: Issue

1 correct
correct
incorrect

2 **Group 1 (subject area)**
economic issues
moral issues
environmental issues
political issue
ethical issues
racial issues

Group 2 (type/importance)
key issues
explosive issues
important issue
particular issue
central issue
complex issues
contentious issue
minor issue
main issues
current issue

Group 3 (quantity)
single issue
another issue

3 issue *for*
issue *in*
issue *of*

4 the issue for *all of us*
the issue for *each patient*
the issue for *debate*
the issue for *consideration*

the issue in *cell differentiation*
the issue in *textual and sexual theory*

the issue in *Canada*
the issue in *the early years of the war*
the issue in *contemporary human affairs*

the issue of *contention*
the issue of *class conflict*
the issue of *the year*
the issue of *climate change*
the issue of *economic progress*
the issue of *the social worth of sport*
the issue of *the freedom of the individual*

5 the issue *for* (people affected)
the issue *of* (specific topics)
the issue *in* (a topic containing more than one issue)
the issue *in, of* (time/place)
the issue *for* (thought/speech)

6 **a** religious
b raises, of
c to resolve, particular
d of, for
e central
f of
g of

7 (suggested answers)
• Discussion regarding the legalisation of marijuana often revolves around the issue of whether or not consumption of marijuana is likely to lead to the consumption of more dangerous drugs.

• Complex moral and religious issues are involved in the controversy surrounding euthanasia.

• Environmentalists have referred to forest exploitation as an example of the government's lack of concern about long term issues.

Part 2: Factor

1 correct
incorrect
incorrect

2 **Group 1 (subject area)**
social factors
biological factors
economic factors

Group 2 (type)
similar factors
aggravating factor
contextual factors
common factor
external factors
internal factor
other factors
contributory factor

Group 3 (quality/importance)
important factor
predominant factor
vital factor
irrelevant factors

Group 4 (quantity)
many factors
additional factors
another factor
the only factors
single factor
several factors

3 factor/s *in*

4 factors that *can distort the results*
factors that *might act by influencing*
factors that *caused him to want to continue living*

factors which *together create a predisposition*
factors which *help to prolong this period*

5　a　factors
　　b　issues, issue
　　c　issue
　　d　factors
　　e　factors
　　f　issues
　　g　factors
　　h　issue
　　i　issue, factors

6　(suggested answers)
- In tropical countries deforestation is caused by a combination of factors which can be seen to be related to poverty and government policies attempting to deal with this poverty. Governments encourage the cutting down of trees, or logging, in order to repay their foreign debts, since there is a demand for timber in developed countries. Logging also provides employment and creates open areas for settlement and agriculture, both of these being seen as necessary in overpopulated, developing countries.
- Some important factors which contribute to ill-health in remote communities include lack of readily available medical attention, the expense involved in supplying such isolated communities with a wide range of pharmaceuticals and the difficult physical conditions among which people live.
- The most obvious factor contributing to poverty in developing countries is overpopulation. This results in unemployment which is exacerbated by lack of opportunities for adequate education and training.

Part 3: Concept

1　correct
　　correct
　　incorrect

2　*to form* a concept
　　to defend a concept
　　found in the concept
　　adding up to the concept
　　identifies three other concepts
　　believe that concepts
　　surrounding the concept
　　reinforce this concept
　　developed no general concept

3　*common* concepts
　　definite concept
　　general concept
　　legal concept
　　mental concept
　　mentalist concept
　　modern concept
　　other concepts
　　temporal concept
　　tree-planting concept

4　concept *of*

5　a concept of *one's own identity*
　　a concept of *political freedom*
　　a concept of *time*
　　a concept of *progress*
　　a concept of *history*
　　a concept of *the evolutionary stable strategy*
　　a concept of *freedom*
　　a concept of *inspiration*
　　a concept of *the national entity*
　　a concept of *core membership*
　　a concept of *God and Nature*
　　a concept of *adultery*
　　a concept of *justice*
　　a concept of *number*
　　a concept of *natural selection*
　　a concept of *marriage*
　　a concept of *political economy*

6　a　modern
　　b　to form
　　c　mental
　　d　to defend
　　e　new, legal
　　f　definite

7
- Piaget does not believe that concepts take their origin from linguistic structures.
- The other single most important factor responsible for raising the standard of care was the recognition of venereology as a clinical specialty in its own right.
- The issue here is whether provocation should remain a qualified defence to murder and, if so, how far it should extend.
- Another unifying principle is said to be the concept of trust. This, it is said, is the key factor governing the doctor-patient relationship.
- Where the concepts of God and Nature used to evoke a poetic response in the nineteenth-century reader, the modern poets rely on sex and myth to produce the same effect.
- With the conduct of hostilities the paramount concern for both the USA and Britain, civil aviation remained a minor issue in the early years of the war.

8　(suggested introduction)
- The problem of deforestation in developing countries is an issue causing worldwide alarm, particularly in the light of evidence of global warming. Research also indicates that some birds, animals and insects dependent on forests are in danger of extinction, and plants containing valuable medicinal properties are disappearing. Factors which contribute to deforestation in these countries include overpopulation, poverty, foreign debt and the need for agricultural expansion. There is also a worldwide demand for timber, which makes logging profitable. The concept of the responsibility of already developed countries for environmental issues has led some writers to argue that

richer countries should subsidise developing countries to maintain their forests for the benefit of all. This essay will indicate why it is vital for them to do so.

Unit 2

Part 1: Evidence

1 correct
incorrect*
incorrect
incorrect
*Note: One study may be considered evidence, but **evidence** is a broader concept than just one study.

2 correct
incorrect
incorrect

3 **Group 1 (type/quality)**
conclusive evidence
material evidence
experimental evidence
scientific evidence
clear evidence
good evidence
categorical evidence
available evidence

Group 2 (quantity)
enough evidence
some evidence
no evidence

Group 3 (time sequence)
recent evidence
present evidence

4 *provide* evidence
is/is not evidence
gives evidence
demanded evidence
show evidence
there is/is not evidence
look for evidence
based on evidence

evidence *bearing (upon)*
evidence *comes (from)*
evidence *concerning*
evidence *may consist (of)*
evidence *may be*
evidence *to convict* *
evidence *to suggest* *
*Notice that *to convict, to suggest* are non-finite verbs.

5 evidence *for*
evidence *from*
evidence *of*
evidence *on*

6 evidence *of*
evidence *for*
evidence *on*
evidence *from*

7 a to suggest
b of, comes
c of, may be
d that
e may consist
f that
g that
h of
i provide
j that

8 (suggested answers)
• Evidence from Australia indicates that the Greek language has been successfully maintained.

• There is evidence that physical contact by the therapist can prevent self-cutting.

Part 2: Research

1 correct
incorrect
incorrect*
correct
*Note: One study that has been done can be considered research, but the term **research** refers to a wider concept, of which a single study may form a part.

2 He had created a research laboratory and clinic.

3 • Wrangham's (1975, 1977) research at the Gombe Stream reserve

• recent research by Olwyn Rasa (1977)

• Brosset's (1978) research on the Malimbus weavers

4 The date of publication of a particular piece of research

5 correct
correct
incorrect*
correct
*You could, however, say 'a piece of research' or 'a research study'.

6 research *about the past*
research *at the Gombe Stream reserve*
research *by Olwyn Rasa*
research *in environmental problems*
research *into non-intensive methods of agriculture*
research *of the great ecologist David Lack*
research *on the Malimbus weavers*
research *during the 1990s*

7 the broad subject area
the broad subject area
the topic/the broad subject area
the topic
the person
the person
the place
the time

8 **Group 1 (type)**
historical research
international research
such research
aesthetic research
comparative research
scientific research

Group 2 (quantity)
additional research
further research
no research

Group 3 (time)
recent research

9 research *might be undertaken*
research *has shown*
research *indicates*
research *might pursue*
research *is continuing*
research *shows*
research *will tell*

10 a evidence
b research
c research
d evidence
e research
f research
g evidence
h research

11 • In summary, there is **evidence** that high appreciation of one's language and culture does not necessarily correlate with the desire to maintain that language. This is supported by **research** carried out in Ireland, Greece and North Africa.

• MacKinnon's (1974) **research** produced **evidence** that orang-utans followed the largest calling male.

Part 3: Source

1 Group 2
Group 1
Group 3

2 correct
correct

3 **Group 1 (supplier of information)**
anthropological sources
various sources

only source
major source
main source

Group 2 (origin)
actual source
possible source
sole sources
another source
all source
common sources

Group 3 (provider)
plant sources
food source
protein sources
good sources
animal sources
energy source
methane sources
only source
immediate source

4 a animal
b energy
c only
d possible
e another
f plant/plant/plant
g principal

5 research
evidence
source

6 • Recent research indicates that the slim person is not necessarily eating in a way to promote maximum health.

• There are still further possible sources of deforestation, these being atmospheric and climatic in nature.

• We have already seen, however, that on present evidence, such a process of group selection seems unlikely to be important in evolution.

• These are a main source for our knowledge of the history of deforestation.

• His source is the research of the historian and sociologist Tony Ashworth.

• While much more research needs to be done, enough is known to make preliminary suggestions.

• More conclusive evidence comes from experiments in which the nucleus is removed from a fertilised egg.

7 evidence
evidence
research
research
source
research
source
research
source
research
research
sources

8 (suggested answers)
• The source of Owen's poem may have been an old Welsh poem.

• Box (1987) has summarised the research on the relationship between unemployment, crime and disorder.

• Marx used Prescott as a source on 'Asiatic' production.

• There is some evidence to suggest that contextual clues are needed for retrieval of effects of initial conditioning.

• The main source of information for this chapter was a survey of the recent literature.

Unit 3

Part 1: According to

1 incorrect
correct
correct
incorrect
correct
correct
incorrect
correct

2 Group 1 (person)
according to *a Sumerian poet*
according to *Axelrod and Hamilton*
according to *Bacon*
according to *Berkeley*
according to *Bernard*
according to *Coatney*
according to *Engels*
according to *him*
according to *his biographer Rawley*
according to *Locke*
according to *World Bank figures*
according to *Morgan and Engels*
according to *the historian Polybius*
according to *the Iranian scholar S.H. Taquizadah*
according to *the theologian O. Cullman*

Group 2 (theory/view)
according to *a basically Aristotelian view*
according to *classical myth*
according to *early Jewish and Christian legend*
according to *Islamic tradition*
according to *such a theory*
according to *the general theory*
according to *the science of optics*
according to *this alternative view*

Group 3 (document/report)
according to *American surveys*
according to *Asser's Life of King Alfred*
according to *one calculation*

according to *one report*
according to *recent polar ice-core studies*
according to *the account presented above*
according to *the survey's findings*

3 people

4 incorrect
incorrect
correct
correct
correct
correct
incorrect

5 **b** According to classical myth, Hercules set the pillars up at the Straits of Gibraltar.
or
Hercules set the pillars up at the Straits of Gibraltar, according to classical myth.
or
Hercules, according to classical myth, set the pillars up at the Straits of Gibraltar.

c According to recent polar ice-core studies, methane's concentration in the atmosphere in 1990 was more than twice as high as occurred in previous interglacial periods.
or
Methane's concentration in the atmosphere in 1990 was more than twice as high as occurred in previous interglacial periods, according to recent polar ice-core studies.
or
Methane's concentration in the atmosphere in 1990 was, according to recent polar ice-core studies, more than twice as high as occurred in previous interglacial periods.

6 (suggested answers)
• According to Leggett (1990), 50 billion tonnes of minerals are mined from the earth each year.

• A doctor, according to Kennedy (1988) is primarily bound to listen to his patient's wishes and to respect them.

Part 2: Claim

1 correct
incorrect
incorrect
correct
incorrect

2 that

3 Locke's claim that
The Führer's claim that
Weissman's claim

4 incorrect
correct
incorrect

5 • We may now consider a paper of Stoyanov (1979) in which he claimed to have obtained a solution without singularities.

• He had an exalted idea of history that is well illustrated by his claim that the historian's duty is 'to rejudge the conduct of men, that generous actions may be snatched from oblivion'.

• Such self-organisation of a coordinate system was, he claimed, quite beyond conventional science, and required a special biological force.

• The phrase seems to have originated in the world of baseball, although some authorities claim priority for an alternative connotation.

• Certainly, he is denying the world of the philosophers, a world of objects beyond direct perception. But he is not, he claims, denying the world of common sense, not denying the reality of a world of directly perceived objects.

6 **a** According to
b claimed/claimed that
c according to
d claimed that

e claimed to
f according to
g claimed/claimed that

7 (suggested answers)
- Murray (1994) claimed that the framing of the photographs made the style of the painting difficult to analyse.
- Waddington (1989) claimed that Canadians are closer to the Victorian traditions of gentility than we imagine.
- Ashcroft and Ashcroft (1989) claim that one can lose weight without lowering one's metabolic rate.

8 The first sentence tells in a completely neutral way what the thesis states. The second sentence indicates that the thesis is adamant about this statement (which may or may not be true).

9 (suggested answers)
a The Catholic church claims that contraception is against the law of God, however it is the most reliable means of controlling population growth.

b Brown claims to have found a cure for cancer, but the food and drug laws of the country have not yet approved of this medication.

10 a According to Johnson's claim, the water in Wamberal lake is contaminated, but children continue to swim there without ill effects.

b The claim that cats produce an antiseptic in their saliva is, according to some veterinary surgeons, correct, however it is wise to teach children to wash their hands after playing with a cat.

Part 3: Suggest

1 correct
correct

incorrect
incorrect
correct
correct
correct

2 that
by

3
- Trivers goes so far as to suggest that many of our psychological characteristics – envy, guilt, gratitude, sympathy etc – have been shaped by natural selection for improved ability to cheat.
- D.B. MacDonald has speculated on the difficult question of the origin of this view in Islam and has suggested that it arose from a Muslim heresy.
- Alongside the standard sanitary admonitions of scientific management, Gray suggested improvements that would ease the housewife's workday and strain.
- What all this work suggests is that the human's body clock and rhythms show several periods and that the combination of life-style and environment tends to accentuate one of these.
- Bernheim's results suggested that he had found some substances which were good for tubercle bacilli.
- In the United States reports have suggested that up to 50 per cent of cases of gonorrhoea in males may be symptomless.
- It has been suggested that sleep is a time when brain activity changes from one of acquiring, interpreting, and acting upon information obtained from the environment to one of consolidating daytime memories.

4 a suggested
b claim
c suggested
d According to

e claim
f according to
g suggested
h suggested
i claim
j According to

5 (suggested answers)
a According to Brown, the lake is contaminated but this may not be cause for closing the lake to swimmers because children swim there without ill effect.

b According to veterinary surgeons, cats produce an antiseptic with their saliva and this appears to be true because they heal their wounds by licking them.

c This book suggests that money is the root of all evil but it should only be dangerous when used unwisely.

d This student suggests that there are important cultural differences regarding expectations of academic writing and there is considerable evidence to support this idea.

e Brown claims that inner-city living is unhealthy but many who live in these areas would disagree.

f Ehrlich's claim that the world's population is exploding is widely accepted and statistics in many countries provide evidence that this is true.

6
- Hall (1991) suggests that contextual stimuli may be able to interact with a particular pattern of nervous activity.
- Crook (1985) claims that efficiency in competition is a very important source of selection, occurring in various areas of social life.
- Whitrow (1990) suggests that the red ochre which covered the bodies may have been associated with blood, in the hope of warding off death.

- According to Hawton and Catalan (1990) these factors can be assessed by encouraging a family to discuss a current issue.
- Kennedy (1988) claims that the proper criteria can only be identified by considering medical treatment in two categories.

7 (suggested answers)

a According to the report, adequate safeguards and standards were clearly necessary.

b He claims that that there are also molecular changes occurring which are not selected, because they have little or no effect on function. The view is still controversial, but I think it is winning.

c According to Greenpeace the goal must be elimination of fossil fuels from the energy inventory, and that that goal should be reflected in the target for the year 2000.

d I would suggest that these exceptions are so infrequent that they are not a reason for abandoning the neo-Darwinist mechanism as the one which underlies the vast majority of adaptive evolutionary changes.

Unit 4

Part 1: Identification

1 correct
correct
correct
correct
incorrect

2 identification *of*

3 *the facts are* identified
attitudes are identified
a linguistic form is identified

Another of many criteria is identified*
time is identified
Greek literature is identified
carcinogens are identified
it is identified
sugar is identified
factors are identified
bacteria are identified
stages in the life cycle are identified
eight hundred buildings are identified
*Note: Although *criteria* is plural, *Another of many criteria* refers to one criterion.

4 we identified two characteristics
a later Muslim tradition identified the Rock

5 correct
correct
correct

6 a identified
b identification
c identified
d identify
e identifiable
f identification
g identifiable, identify
h identify
i identifying

7 (suggested sentence)
Hall (1991) identified a number of interference theories which may explain latent inhibition.

Part 2: Analysis

1 correct
incorrect
correct
incorrect

2 Group 1 (subject area)
sociological analysis
ethical analysis
political analysis
historical analysis

Group 2 (type/quality)
theoretical analysis
conceptual analysis
thorough analysis
objective analysis
subjective analysis
critical analysis
detailed analysis
basic analysis
final analysis
comparative analysis
careful analysis
logical analysis
best-documented analyses

Group 3 (quantity)
any analysis
further analysis

3 analysis *of*

4 analyses

5 a analysis
b identifies
c analysis
d analysed
e identified
f analysed
g Identification
h analysis
i identified
j analysis
k identified

6 (suggested answer)
- In order to analyse the difficulties which many new students experience when commencing university study, it it necessary first to identify these difficulties. They include difficulties involved in becoming part of a new community (the university), such as making new friends, getting to know one's teachers and the physical layout of the university, and becoming accustomed to norms of

behaviour which may be different to those experienced in previous educational settings. Another group of difficulties are those related to the study skills required in a university, including the need for independence and self-motivation, learning more sophisticated research skills, adjusting to the level of difficulty of lectures and reading materials, and becoming familiar with the academic style and vocabulary of the subjects being studied. In the final analysis, the major difficulties new students experience when commencing university study can be seen as being either social or academic.

Part 3: Criteria

1 correct
correct
incorrect
correct
correct

2 **Group 1 (type/quality)**
clear criteria
objective criteria
proper criteria
the same criteria
relevant criteria

Group 2 (subject area)
medical criteria
psychological criteria

Group 3 (quantity)
several criteria
all criteria
two criteria
no criterion
one criterion

3 for
of

4 criteria for *determining sex*
criteria for *distinguishing sexual*

characteristics
criteria for *distinguishing truth*
criterion for *human maturity*
criterion for *admission*
criteria of *excellence*
criterion of *perception*
criterion of *truth*
criterion of *musical phenomena*

5 for
of
for

6 • They had no clear criteria to show where the line was to be drawn.

• The relevant criterion is whether two forms commonly interbreed in the wild, and not whether they can be persuaded to do so in captivity.

• What we have to do is to come up with some set of criteria which relate to the relative value we are prepared, if pressed, to attribute to a particular form of special treatment.

• We can only identify the proper criteria correctly if we accept that medical treatment in general ought to be divided, for our purposes, into two classes.

• This capacity for choice, implicit rather than active in so many people, can in fact be taken as one criterion for human maturity.

• Obviously, purely objective criteria such as the patient's age or the particular illness cannot be justified or relied upon.

• Is there such a thing as a 'criterion' of truth? Do we have any 'instrument' or means of getting at the truth?

7 analysis
criteria
identified

8 (suggested model)
This discussion of the advantages and disadvantages of using public transport will first of all identify some of the more commonly used forms of public transport in present day Australia. It will then suggest various criteria by which the use of public transport can be evaluated. An analysis of the advantages and disadvantages of using public transport will be put forward, followed by the conclusion that the advantages of using public transport definitely outweigh the disadvantages.

In order to identify the means of public transport most frequently used in Australia today, one needs only to spend some time in a large city such as Sydney and its surroundings. Trains, buses and taxis carry the public to and from work and other appointments throughout the day and night. Other forms of public transport such as ferries and aircraft are also used on a daily basis, however since ferries are not a typical form of transport to many parts of Australia, and since relatively few Australians use aircraft as a regular, routine form of transport, this essay will confine itself to considering the advantages and disadvantages of using trains, buses and taxis.

Various criteria need to be taken into account when considering the advantages and disadvantages of using public transport. Among the most important are economic considerations, convenience to the passenger, safety and environmental issues. We will thus evaluate the use of trains, buses and taxis according to these criteria.

The alternative to using public transport is owning and running a private car. The original cost of a car, obligatory insurance, the cost of petrol, repair and maintenance clearly make the use of trains and buses a cheaper alternative, particularly considering the concessions available to schoolchildren, students, pensioners and senior citizens. Taxis are certainly more expensive than trains and buses, and no concessions are available. However considering that they are usually used only for short trips and when trains and buses are not easily available, it can be seen that the use of taxis is probably also cheaper for most people than owning and running a private car.

The second criterion, convenience to passengers, is perhaps one which highlights the main disadvantages of using public transport. The nearest train or bus station may be some distance from one's home or destination, transport may not run as frequently as required and it may be crowded. Taxis are more convenient if one uses them from home or an office where they can be telephoned to arrive at a certain time. However it may be difficult to find a taxi if one does not have access to a telephone or is in an unfamiliar part of a town or city. There are, however, conveniences associated with using public transport related to being a passenger rather than a driver. The passenger is free to relax, read (if not prone to travel sickness) or carry on a conversation without having to concentrate on the demands of the road and traffic. This freedom may thus compensate for some of the inconveniences of using public transport.

The number of car and motor cycle accidents reported daily in Australia is alarming. Although buses, trains and taxis are also occasionally involved in accidents they seem to occur much less frequently. This is probably due to the greater experience and more rigid training conditions of drivers of public transport, along with the requirement that vehicles for public transport be

extremely reliable. It is clear for these reasons that public transport is likely to be safer than driving one's own car.

Environmentalists argue strongly for the promotion of fuel efficient public transport. Individual cars on the road are not only responsible for higher levels of air pollution than would be the case if car owners abandoned use of their cars to share public transport, they are also largely responsible for the rapid rate at which fossil fuels are being depleted. It is obvious that 20 people, for example, travelling from a the city to Macquarie University in a bus will pollute the environment and deplete fossil fuels at a much lower rate than 20 people who travel the same distance in their own cars.

On all criteria except convenience public transport can be seen to have definite advantages over private transport, and there are some conveniences of public transport that may compensate for its occasional lack of accessibility. It is therefore reasonable to conclude that the advantages of using public transport definitely outweigh the disadvantages.

Unit 5

Part 1: May

1 correct
correct
incorrect

2 well

3 may *appear*
may *be*
may *become*
may *expect*
may *find*
may *have*
may *involve*
may *occur*

may *result*
may *seem*

4 it may also be observed that
it may also be noted that
it may be noted that

5 it

6 • Consequently, the doctor may appear to play the role of God, the giver and taker of life.

• It is often better to leave such exploration until the patient's difficulties are beginning to resolve because by then the patient may be more willing to consider, for example, that his act was based on hostile and manipulation motives.

• Plasmids are often symbionts rather than parasites: that is, they benefit rather than injure their hosts, for example by carrying with them properties such as drug resistance which may be of value to the host cell.

• In some cases bodies were covered with red ochre, which may have been intended to simulate blood, in the hope of averting physical extinction.

• An individual may not be able to reach his own head, but nothing is easier than for a friend to do it for him.

• Although the treatment is free, the patient may well be asked to pay for the tests used in diagnosis.

• It may result from inconveniently timed appointments or travel difficulties.

7 (suggested answers)
• In addition, deep lacerations may result in disfiguring scars. The deformity or disfigurement may be an added cause for depression and regret at having failed.

- In a proportion of cases the first site of infection may be the cervix, where there may not be any local pain.

- This alteration may be either excitatory or inhibitory; that is, it may make the receiving cell more or less likely to emit impulses itself.

Part 2: Possible

1 Group 2
Group 1
Group 3

2 Group 3

3 possible *solution*
possible *bases*
possible *objections*
possible *means*
possible *method*
possible *risks*

4 possible to *eliminate*
possible to *lose*
possible to *point to*
possible to *analyse*
possible to *discover*
possible to *introduce*
possible to *catch up on*
possible to *proceed*
possible to *conceive*
possible to *determine*
possible to *adopt*

5 *it should be* possible
it is possible
(progress) is often made possible
just beginning to make possible
it is not possible
it is now possible
it is often possible
it is theoretically possible
it was possible
it becomes possible
it is still possible

6 **a** solution
b that
c to lose
d to point
e means
f risks
g for

7 possible
may
may
may
possible
possible
may
possible
possible
may
may
may
possible
possible

8 (suggested answers)
- It is possible for sentiments of approval of a violent past to coexist with abhorrence for most current acts of violence.

- One possible means of reconciling the new right and Thatcherism to the conservative tradition would be to abandon the emphasis on 'authority' and emphasise the duality of Conservative thought.

Part 3: Unlikely

1 incorrect
correct
incorrect

2 *clearly* unlikely
very unlikely
extremely unlikely
most unlikely
highly unlikely
not unlikely

3 *seem* unlikely
considered unlikely
is unlikely
make (it) unlikely
was unlikely
looked unlikely

unlikely *to cause*
unlikely *to be eaten*
unlikely *to prove*
unlikely *to be able to*
unlikely *to succeed*
unlikely *to change*
unlikely *to match*
unlikely *to be (the same)*
unlikely *to provide*
unlikely *to improve*
unlikely *to be overlooked*
unlikely *to be altered*
unlikely *to be discovered*
unlikely *to produce*

4 unlikely *that*
unlikely *to*

5 unlikely *event*
unlikely *trainer*
unlikely *truth*

6 - As regards property, it should be noticed that law and practice, to a large extent, make it unlikely that property of any considerable value will come into the direct ownership of an infant.

- It seems unlikely that herds in developing countries can long continue to expand, given the already serious problems from over-grazing and desertification.

- If society in all its aspects has always been in a state of flux, it is highly unlikely that this process will end at any particular time.

- Although the symptoms displayed by the patient usually relate to terminal illness, there may be times when they arise from some separate, independent condition.

- It is possible to point to several cases of reversal.

- Cancer is not one disease but many, and the answers are unlikely to be the same for all of them.

- He thought she had shown moderate suicidal intent in taking the overdose, particularly because she took it at night when unlikely to be discovered and repeated the act on waking in the morning.

- Teaching at night is unlikely to prove popular (with teacher or pupil) and the night shift in a hospital ward cannot be made equivalent to the day shift (except in intensive care units which are continuously busy).

7 a possible
b may
c unlikely
d may
e possible
f unlikely
g unlikely
h may
i unlikely
j unlikely

8 (suggested answer)
Since patients may have different reactions to the various methods of administering this drug, it is unlikely that any one method would suit all patients.

Part 4: Probably

1 correct
incorrect
incorrect

2 *most* probably
very probably

3 probably *never*
probably *not*

4 it

5 a become
b that
c came
d that
e to be altered
f reflected
g to lose
h that
i occurred
j to discover
k depended
l to prove

6 Group 1 unlikely
Group 2 probably
Group 3 may
Group 4 possible

7 *Ramapithecus* was one of several primates, such as the baboons, which came down from the trees to develop terrestrial living. Its dental adaptations to hard savannah fruits and seeds <u>probably</u> preceded the development of bipedalism, which <u>may</u> itself have been originally connected with foraging, reaching upward to browse on bushes for example. *Ramapithecus* lasted for about 7 million years and <u>may</u> have then given rise to the first true hominid, *Australopithecus*, which has a similar dental structure. *Ramapithecus* <u>may</u> not have been carnivorous, and the association between hunting, travel, and bipedalism <u>probably</u> emerged only with the true hominids.

8 **Very sure**
must
almost certain
most probably

Fairly sure
often possible
likely
probable

may well
could well
probably
should be possible

Not very sure
possible, though unlikely,
seems unlikely

Very doubtful
extremely unlikely
most unlikely
not possible in general

9 (suggested answer)
Ownership of Computers and Modems in the Australian Home

Although these results come from a small-scale study and one therefore cannot make definite generalisations for Australia as a whole, they may indicate certain trends in ownership of computers and modems in Australia. Results suggest that ownership of both computers and modems increased steadily during 1995, and that by December of that year half of all Australian households may have owned a personal computer. There was a possible increase of about 10 per cent in computer ownership in 1995, and there appears to have been an even more rapid growth in modem ownership, results indicating a possible doubling of households owning modems during the year 1995. It is, however, most unlikely that even half the owners of personal computers also own modems. Under present circumstances it seems probable that this increase in computer and modem ownership will continue in future years.

Unit 6

Part 1: Concluding

1 particularly tentative 5, 14, 22, 28, 31
particularly definite   8, 11, 16, 20, 37

2 • It would be premature to conclude

• Our provisional conclusion can be no more than

• It is perhaps too early to reach a conclusion on this point

3 • We are forced to conclude

• It must be concluded

• I feel that there can be only one conclusion

4 • It is reasonable to conclude

• It is not unreasonable, then, to conclude

• It is therefore reasonable to conclude

5 • Our provisional conclusion can be no more than that

• It is enough to prompt the tentative conclusion that

6 therefore
thus
then

7 *provisional* conclusion
main conclusion
tentative conclusion
chief conclusion
natural conclusion
certain conclusion

8 provisional
tentative

9 incorrect
correct
correct
correct
incorrect

10 a conclusion
b conclude
c conclusions
d conclude
e concluded
f conclusion

11 (suggested answer)
It can therefore be concluded that poverty and overpopulation are underlying causes of deforestation in tropical countries.

12 (suggested answer)
Although the experimental evidence that watching television violence promotes antisocial behaviour is not strong, the hypothesis is supported by observations of parents and teachers intimately involved with children. There is also evidence that watching violent news programs can affect the perceptions of children regarding levels of violence in their own neighbourhood, which presumably influence their behaviour. It can therefore be concluded that, although further research is needed in order to make a more definitive statement, it is very likely that watching television violence affects children's behaviour.

Part 2: Summarising

1 correct
correct

2 • It may help if I summarise the main conclusions

• I will now try to summarise what I have said

• To summarise

• If I were to summarise

• In summary, then,

• Thus, in summary

3 thus
then

4 incorrect
correct
correct
incorrect

5 a conclude
b summarise
c conclude
d summarise
e conclude

6 (suggested answer)
I will now attempt to summarise the main differences between a conclusion and a summary. A conclusion expresses the writer's own reflection on information that has been presented, whereas a summary is either a brief listing of points that have been presented in more complete form or a concise statement which provides that information in a nutshell. A conclusion can be stated tentatively, fairly definitely or very definitely whereas a summary is usually unquestioned. And finally, the words conclude and conclusion are often followed by that, which is not the case for the words summarise and summary.

7 (suggested answer)
To summarise the above table, Australian children spend their money in slightly different ways according to gender. Boys spend most of their money on toys and games, followed in descending order by spending on sweets, sports and hobbies, computer and video games, savings, books, going out, presents and clothes. Girls, on the other hand, spend most of their money on sweets, followed by toys and games, books, clothes, presents, going out, savings, tapes and CDs, sports and hobbies and video games.

Part 3: Clear that

1 correct

incorrect
correct
correct
incorrect
correct

2 **a** clear that
    b conclusion
    c conclusion
    d thus
    e summarise, conclusions
    f Thus, clear that
    g conclusion
    h summarise
    i clear that
    j conclusion
    k clear that, conclusion
    l clear that
    m summarise
    n clear that
    o conclusion
    p Thus, conclusion

3 clear that
    conclude
    summary
    thus

4 (suggested answer)
Having considered the arguments for and against the cultivation of tobacco, it must be concluded that the problems associated with consumption of tobacco make it economically untenable as a form of agriculture. Despite arguments that the cultivation of tobacco benefits small farmers, businesses and governments and that it provides rural employment, the cost to government, individuals and production in general through smoking-related illnesses more than eliminate any possible economic advantages.

References

Microconcord references

The references used throughout this book are listed here as they appear in the listing for MicroConcord Corpus Collection B. All titles listed here are published by Oxford University Press.

Arts

Apartment Seven: Essays Selected and New, Miriam Waddington, OUP: Canada (1989). Literary criticism, anecdotes.

Toulouse-Lautrec; Formative Years 1878–91, G. Murray, OUP (forthcoming). Biography.

Wilfred Owen, Jon Stallworthy, OUP (1977). Biography of the poet.

Belief and religion

Marxism and Anthropology, Maurice Bloch, OUP (1984). Analysis of the relationship between Marxism and anthropology.

The Empiricists, R.S. Woolhouse, OUP (1988). Study of Locke, Berkeley, Hume, etc.

The History of Christianity, John McManners (ed), OUP (1990). Reference book.

The Morality of Freedom, J. Raz, OUP (1986). Philosophy.

Applied science

Your Body Clock, J.M. Waterhouse, D.S. Minors, M.E. Waterhouse, OUP (1990). Popular physiology.

Get Slim and Stay Slim: The Psychology of Weight Control, Jennifer Ashcroft and J. Barrie Ashcroft, OUP (1989). Proposals for healthy eating, weight control and exercise.

Perceptual and Associative Learning, Geoffrey Hall, OUP (1991). Psychology and cognitive theory.

Sexually Transmitted Diseases: The Facts, David Barlow, OUP (1979). Medical textbook.

Attempted Suicide. A Practical Guide to its Nature and Management, Keith Hawton and Jose Catalan, OUP (1990).

Treat Me Right, Ian Kennedy, OUP (1988). Essays in medical; law and ethics.

Science

The Evolution of Human Consciousness, John H. Crook, OUP (1985). Social biology.

Global Warming: The Greenpeace Report, Ed. Jeremy Leggett, OUP (1990). Papers on the green house threat by scientists and energy analysts.

The Problems of Biology, John Maynard Smith, OUP (1989). Introduction of biology, especially molecular genetics.

The Selfish Gene, Richard Dawkins, OUP (1985). Social biology and evolution.

Time in History, G.J. Whitrow, OUP (1990). Analysis of concepts of time, history and evolution.

Social science

20th Century British History, Vol. 2 No 1, OUP (1991). Academic history periodical.

Tackling the Inner Cities, Susanne MacGregor and Ben Pimlott, OUP (1991). Analysis of effects of Thatcherism on the inner cities.

Other references

Bush, D., K. Cadman, P. de Lacy, D. Simmons and J. Thurstun. 1996. 'Expectations of academic writing at Australian universities': work in progress. Paper presented at the *First National Conference on Tertiary Literacy*, Melbourne, 15–16 March 1996.

McCarthy, M. and F. O'Dell. 1994. *English Vocabulary in Use*. Cambridge: Cambridge University Press.

Thurstun, J. 1993, *Maintenance of the Spanish language as reflected by adolescents of Chilean, Peruvian and Spanish background in Sydney*. MA dissertation. Macquarie University.